VIENNA

By David Pryce-Jones
and the Editors of Time-Life Books

Photographs by Thomas Höpker

THE GREAT CITIES · TIME-LIFE BOOKS · AMSTERDAM

The Author: David Pryce-Jones was born in Vienna in 1936. He was educated in England at Eton and Magdalen College, Oxford, and subsequently taught creative writing at the University of Iowa and the University of California at Berkeley in the United States. His books include a history of the 1956 Hungarian Uprising; a novel, *The Stranger's View*, set in the Vienna of that period; and a biography entitled *Unity Mitford, A Quest.*

The Photographer: Thomas Höpker was born in Munich in 1936. He studied the history of art at Munich University and has worked as a photo-journalist since 1961, including five years on the staff of *Stern* magazine. His photographs have been frequently exhibited and four volumes of his work have been published. He has also made documentary films for German television.

TIME-LIFE INTERNATIONAL
EUROPEAN EDITOR: George Constable
Assistant European Editor: Kit van Tulleken
Design Consultant: Louis Klein
Chief Designer: Graham Davis
Director of Photography: Pamela Marke

THE GREAT CITIES
Editorial Staff for *Vienna*
Editor: Simon Rigge
Designer: Eric Molden
Picture Editor: Gunn Brinson
Staff Writers: Tony Allan, Mike Brown
Text Researcher: Liz Goodman
Design Assistant: Derek Copsey

Editorial Production
Production Editor: Ellen Brush
Art Department: Julia West
Editorial Department: Ajaib Singh Gill
Picture Department: Lynn Farr, Thelma Gilbert, Gina Marfell

The captions and the texts accompanying the photographs in this volume were prepared by the editors of TIME-LIFE Books.

Valuable assistance was given in the preparation of this volume by the TIME-LIFE Correspondent in Vienna, Gertraud Lessing.

Published by TIME-LIFE International (Nederland) B.V.
Ottho Heldringstraat 5, Amsterdam 1018.

Cover: Seen through the embroidered lace curtains of an Albertinaplatz coffee-house, an equestrian statue of the Archduke Albrecht—a 19th-Century Austrian military hero—is silhouetted against the evening sky.

First end paper: The midday sun lights up a grove of young beeches in the Vienna Woods, the forested hills that lie to the west of the city, where the Alps drop down to the Danube. For generations these woods have been a favourite haunt of Viennese in search of peace and relaxation.

Last end paper: At one of Vienna's *Heurigen*—country taverns where recently matured wine is sold on the grower's premises—chairs and tables are tipped at the end of the day to shed rain.

Contents

I

A City Ruled by the Past

The 210-foot-high Ferris wheel in the Prater amusement park, standing behind the tracks and girders of the adjacent roller coaster, was built in 1897 as an expression of faith in technology and progress under Habsburg rule. Damaged in the Second World War, it was subsequently repaired, and remains a familiar and symbolic landmark in Vienna.

Vienna, you say to yourself, and a bright light switches on in the mind. Are you not a little bit more relaxed than you were, readier to let yourself go? Aren't your thoughts centred upon cream cakes and light violin music and the general frou-frou of a city given up to pleasure? This notional Vienna exists as a state of mind to which most people are happy to submit themselves. For Vienna is a prime feature of European fairyland, sparkier than the Eternal City of Rome, within sporting distance of Gay Paree, sharing boundaries with the Ruritania of fiction and operetta, the happy Central European state that never was.

I remember as a child being informed that the Viennese waltzed only with their legs, their shoulders remaining so immobile in the dance that teacups could be balanced on them. That's the kind of talk that gives a city its image in the eyes of the world. To many foreigners, the archetype of the successful Londoner still wears a frock-coat and top hat. The Parisian is in white tie and tails, bending to quiz a little dancer, just as a Venetian must be in his gondola. And the Viennese aristocrat steps forward in a white uniform never designed for battle, the trousers skin-tight, the collar a choker high up under the chin, his chest a-glitter with discreetly matching orders and decorations. His expression is grave, with a hint of irresponsibility in the eyes. His shoulders are well-squared. His wife, in a silk or satin dress, is beautiful and soft and good and modest.

They simply will not fade away, this pair, whose faces stare back at us from some strategic point in all the museums and palaces of Vienna. Yes, they seem to be saying, their lives were extraordinarily privileged in what had been a greater capital than Berlin or St. Petersburg—centre of a continental empire that in their time stretched right across Central Europe from the borders of Germany almost to the Black Sea. But they seek to defend nothing; they have neither regrets nor excuses, being far too self-confident and good-humoured ever to moralize. While the going was good, they were happy, carefree, elegant, and there is no more to be said.

The tourists come now to the capital of nothing more than a small neutral country. They come by the coachload from Japan and America and Scandinavia and even Communist Europe, having in common that imagined vista of a ball-room where the music and dancing and sweetness and light and Mozart go on for ever and ever. You see the visitors' baffled holiday-faces pressing against the triplex glass of air-conditioned buses, and their cameras click away like so many crickets on a summer night. Then you realize that they have come on a search for the sense of living gaiety which is not in themselves, and which therefore they will never find. That is not Vienna's fault.

More than 20 years ago I drove to Vienna along the autobahn from Germany, where I was serving as a National Service soldier in the British Army. I was a brash 18-year-old with a few days' local leave. I too was looking for a sense of gaiety, and perhaps for past links; for I had been born in this city just a couple of years before Hitler destroyed whatever was left of the old civilization. What I found was the ugly spectre of the present.

Since the end of the Second World War, Vienna, like Berlin, had been under an Allied Control Commission composed of the four occupation powers—Britain, France, the United States, the Soviet Union—each of which had carved out a claim to a zone. (Even today, the word for these occupying powers, *Besatzungsmächte*, is uttered with a slight lift of the eyebrows and a hint of a grimace to convey the nuances of a subject impossible to discuss properly, something like a horrible plague from which there was a deathbed recovery.) The headquarters of the four occupying powers was in a large 19th-Century building on the corner of the central and imposing street, the Heumarkt, as though to remind those in the embassies and grand houses of the district what the score now was. Military Jeeps buzzed about outside, roaring off with complete disregard for the rules of the road. The army train that ran regularly to and from England had the enigmatic code name of Medloc and practically everybody who ever took it seemed to have thrived on miserable little bargains on the black market—or more exactly, on street corners where baby-faced touts peddled whisky and cigarettes and silk stockings.

A thriller come to life, in short, and so Graham Greene described it with snapshot clarity in his novel *The Third Man*, that classic of this brief occupation period. His hero, Rollo Martins, at one point walked along the banks of the Danube Canal: "across the water lay the half destroyed Diana baths and in the distance the great black circle of the Prater wheel, stationary above the ruined houses. Over there across the grey water was the second Bezirk, in Russian ownership. St. Stefanskirche shot its enormous wounded spire into the sky above the Inner City, and, coming up the Kärntnerstrasse, Martins passed the lit door of the Military Police station. The four men of the International Patrol were climbing into their Jeep; the Russian M.P. sat beside the driver (for the Russians had that day taken over the chair for the next four weeks) and the Englishman, the Frenchman and the American mounted behind."

That was just how it was. On the weekend of my visit, the Soviet officials had been mounting a ceremonial parade somehow connected with taking over the chair of the Control Commission for their stint. Past the headquarters building on the Heumarkt, they marched into the adjoining square, formerly called the Schwarzenbergplatz but renamed the Stalinplatz by the Russians. At one end was a bronze equestrian statue of Karl

Behind the water-jets of the Schwarzenbergplatz fountain, the bronze image of a Soviet soldier on top of the 65-foot column of the Red Army Monument incongruously holds a shield belonging to another age. Erected in 1945, the monument is an uncomfortable reminder of 10 years of Soviet influence during the four-power occupation of the city after the war.

Philipp Schwarzenberg, Field Marshal of the Habsburg armies during the Napoleonic Wars. At the other end was (still is) a thin spike of a column topped with the effigy of a Soviet soldier as liberator; his likeness was to be found at all points east: in Budapest, Bucharest, Sofia, Warsaw, Riga. To joke about this symbol, as the Viennese did, by calling it "The Unknown Plunderer" (because the Soviets looted everything down to the lavatory seats) or "The Pea King" (on the grounds that the Soviets enforced a diet of dried peas on the population of their zone), was poor consolation. The façade of the 18th-Century Schwarzenberg Palace in the background suffered from that special drabness which comes with neglect; it was as grey as a warehouse. As the close-ranked Russians marched, swinging their jackboots up and thumping them down, they held their rifles stiff and vertical at the side, bayonets fixed; with the march's movement those bayonets flashed up and down, perilously, for if someone closed in a centimetre too near to the man in front, he risked transfixing his comrade right between the shoulder blades. Uniforms were slashed continually.

Anyone who has known those times, I think, has claims to honorary citizenship of Vienna. The 20th Century has not been kind to the city. More than 50 years have passed since this was the proud and glorious capital of the proud and glorious empire of the Habsburgs, the greatest ruling family in all Europe, who had put their personal stamp on the continent's history since the Middle Ages. No more glory now, no more pride—only half a century of loss. The Habsburgs may not rule, but the past does. The collapse of an empire brings instability and fear; people cling to whatever traditions they imagine can tide them over.

When the Habsburg Empire broke up at the end of the First World War, its 50 million citizens suddenly acquired new nationalities. Whole provinces and groups of provinces suddenly became independent countries—

The skyline of central Vienna, as seen from across the Danube Canal, is dominated by the patterned roof and spire of St. Stefan's Cathedral, built 700 years ago. Planning laws, passed in the 1930s, limit the height of new buildings in the Inner City to 85 feet.

Hungary and Czechoslovakia, for example. Other provinces were absorbed into neighbouring states such as Yugoslavia and Romania. As the French Prime Minister Georges Clemenceau said when he signed the peace treaty of Versailles in 1918, whatever was left over was Austria. Fewer than seven million hardcore Austrians remained in the new and independent Republic, over a fifth of them in Vienna. The city thus became a head without a body—top-heavy, purposeless, the capital of nothing, a place for a bureaucracy which had forms to send out but nobody much to fill them in. There were thousands of redundant soldiers and civil servants with claims on the state they had served to the end. Vienna and everybody in it might as well have been simply pensioned off.

It was all very well to be rid of the old structure. That was easy. The Emperor Franz Josef had blundered into war. He had ruled for the entire second half of the 19th Century, much too long to have perceived that the 20th Century was forcing change upon him. His death in 1916 left his heir and great-nephew, the last Emperor Charles, to lose the war and pay the price. The victorious Allies and the new Republican government insisted that the Habsburg family had to go, just like their royal cousins, the German Hohenzollerns. Nothing too violent—that would have been a trifle un-Viennese—but a matter of arrangements, of luggage and packing. The Swiss Guards had died for Louis XVI at their Versailles post in 1792; after the Bolshevik Revolution in 1917 a White Army had fought for Tsar Nicholas II; but on the last day the Emperor Charles spent in his palace in November, 1918, there was nobody left to answer the bell except two sentries and a few courtiers. The Emperor, his wife Zita and six children travelled by private train to exile in Switzerland. Everything about this drama seemed private.

By an accident of fate, the famous Austrian writer Stefan Zweig was coming home from the war, crossing the Swiss-Austrian frontier at Feldkirch just at the moment when the imperial train was briefly halted there. (Poor Stefan Zweig; he was himself to become a refugee from the Nazis, putting an end to himself in 1942 in a hotel in Brazil.) "I recognised behind the plate-glass window of the car the Emperor Charles, last emperor of Austria, standing with his black-clad wife, Empress Zita. I was startled; the last emperor of Austria, heir of the Habsburg dynasty which had ruled for 700 years, was forsaking his realm. . . . The tall serious man at the window was having a last look at the hills and houses, at the people of his land. . . . The gendarmes, the police, the soldiery, were embarrassed and looked abashed because uncertain whether the traditional recognition was still in order, the women hardly dared to look up, all were silent and thus the faint sobbing of the old lady in mourning who had come heaven knows what distance, only to see 'her' emperor once more, was plainly audible. At last, the conductor gave the signal. Everybody started up mechanically, the inexorable instant had come."

Hours after Hitler entered Vienna on March 14, 1938, to set the seal on the annexation of Austria, the Viennese express their rapturous approval by gathering outside a German travel agency to salute a portrait of the Führer. The next day, enthusiasts perched in trees (opposite) for a better view of Hitler's triumphal motorcade through the capital.

Two years later, after twice attempting to return to his former kingdoms, the Emperor Charles was banished to Madeira. There, after only a few months of pathetic, untended exile, he turned his face to the wall and died of the first illness that seized him. With the hereditary Habsburgs dispossessed, Vienna was a tempting prize for anyone who wanted to try to capture it, whether under the flag of socialism, fascism or communism. As for the Viennese, they could never quite be sure who, in this shabby modern twilight of their history, might emerge on the balcony of some fine public building and proclaim himself the new power in the land.

The first Austrian Republic was socialist. Its first Chancellor was Karl Renner. Although he was a man of rather ordinary gifts, there was nobody else who could unite the country. That was the measure of the emptiness of Vienna after its traditional rulers had departed. Between the two wars, in the undistinguished years of the independent Republic, this emptiness and loss was taken for granted. Writers talked of nothing else and suspected the worst. One of the best studies of the period, Edward Crankshaw's *Vienna*, published at the turning-point of 1938, did not have to justify its sub-title *The Image of a Culture in Decline.*

The political vacuum was shortly to be filled. On March 14, 1938, Adolf Hitler entered Vienna. He had shouted loud enough and long enough about uniting Austria and Germany to spare his army the trouble of firing a shot. He drove in a staff-car and took a suite at the Imperial, the smartest, the most aristocratic of hotels. (Richard Wagner, whom Hitler idolized for the Nazi spirit he so shamingly found in the Nibelung opera cycle, used to stay there for the more innocent purpose of attending rehearsals of his works.) For a moment or two, in his triumph, Hitler appeared on the hotel balcony; but he was tired, over-wrought by the weeks of bluff and hysteria that had brought him to this crest of a wave, invading a country in the face of world opinion and getting away with it.

All Vienna seemed delirious. Tens of thousands lined the streets to wave and to cheer. To them, this was not invasion but a meeting of German blood-brothers. The church bells rang. Children flourished bouquets and parents displayed swastika banners and armbands carefully prepared for such an eventuality. Madness swept over the Viennese, and they embraced it. And then began the persecution of all those to whom the Nazis objected on the grounds of politics or race or talent. About 70,000 Viennese were arrested and imprisoned within a matter of weeks. Suicide or emigration were the alternatives available to the best elements in Vienna. Swiftly, even intelligently within the definition of Hitler's policy, Vienna was reduced to being a provincial city, a leaderless reflection of the Nazi ideal. Austria became nothing more than an eastern province of the Greater German Reich, called the Ostmark.

It was a terrible fate, inflicted—what is more—by a native son. Hitler was Austrian-born, brought up to think of Vienna as the centre of the

Pedestrians pick their way through mounds of rubble in a street in the Wieden district, soon after the capture of Vienna by Soviet forces in April, 1945. By the time the Germans had been driven out, some 20 per cent of the city's buildings lay ruined—the result of several months of shelling and heavy Allied air raids.

universe. Those who have hated Vienna—and many have—bring a personal intensity to their feelings, which are those of a disappointed lover, and very few have hated like Hitler. In the early 1900s he had been there as a small-time artist vainly aspiring to admission to the Vienna Academy, living a down-and-out existence in a Refuge for the Roofless in the district of Meidling or in a Home for Men on the Meldemannstrasse. He never forgot nor forgave what he considered to be this spurning of his talent. Not surprisingly, when he returned, he made straight for the Imperial Hotel to show the stuck-up Viennese that he was as good as the best of them, winning at the head of an army the acclaim he felt he had always deserved.

Old Vienna, then, sank without trace; defenceless, abject—especially in its efforts to cling to the shreds of its culture—the city was like some old strip-teaser performing with a transparent veil. By 1945, with the Allied forces drawing nearer all the time, the city could no longer be blind to the consequences of its enthusiastic Nazism. Bombing and war damage were not severe compared with what had happened elsewhere, but to this day the Viennese speak as though they had been through as much as the inhabitants of Rotterdam or Warsaw or even Berlin. As Graham Greene's Martins had seen, the Diana baths, one of Vienna's main swimming pools, had been hit, the Ferris wheel in the huge, once fashionable Prater park had been damaged and the famous Opera House bombed. In the eleventh-hour shelling and hand-to-hand fighting between departing Germans and Marshal Tolbukhin's advancing Soviet troops, a good many outlying districts, or *Bezirke*, were battered.

The last Gauleiter of Vienna, Baldur von Schirach, formerly head of the Hitler Youth movement, left the city early in April, 1945. When he

A portrait of the Soviet leader, with the legend "Glory to the great Stalin", reminds passers-by that they are in the Soviet zone of Vienna, one of four sectors administered by Allied nations after the war. The occupying powers withdrew in 1955, after signing the State Treaty that committed Austria to neutrality.

pulled out of the Hofburg, the ancient imperial court in which he had installed himself, he loaded a score of lorries with loot, but by then the convoy had nowhere to go and fell into the hands of the Americans. One of his colleagues, Dr. Hugo Jury, prepared a final statement urging Austrians not to abandon Nazism, although at the moment it was released, both he and Hitler had already done away with themselves. This sequence of events was in keeping with the immortal spirit of Vienna: it is always too late—or if not, then there's still nothing to be done about it.

So it was that March 14, 1938, came to be repaid; one occupation led to another. Allied generals and Soviet commissars stood on official balconies or parade-ground stands and were watched by surly spectators. In April, 1945, the 74-year-old Karl Renner was called upon to repeat his rescue act of 27 years earlier and form a government that would bring Austria through the uneasy years of threatened partition between eastern and western military blocs. Renner was practised at stepping through wreckage. He had able colleagues and successors, and the second rescue eventually worked far better than the first.

On May 15, 1955, a State Treaty was signed in the Red Marble Room of the Belvedere Palace, built in the first decades of the 18th Century by the great baroque architect Lukas von Hildebrandt. On the ceremonial balcony now stood such very different figures as U.S. Secretary of State John Foster Dulles, Soviet Foreign Minister Vyacheslav Molotov, French Foreign Minister Antoine Pinay and British Foreign Secretary Harold Macmillan. With them stood Julius Raab and Leopold Figl, Chancellor and Foreign Minister of an Austria once more independent. The occupation troops of all four powers were to be withdrawn. There would be no

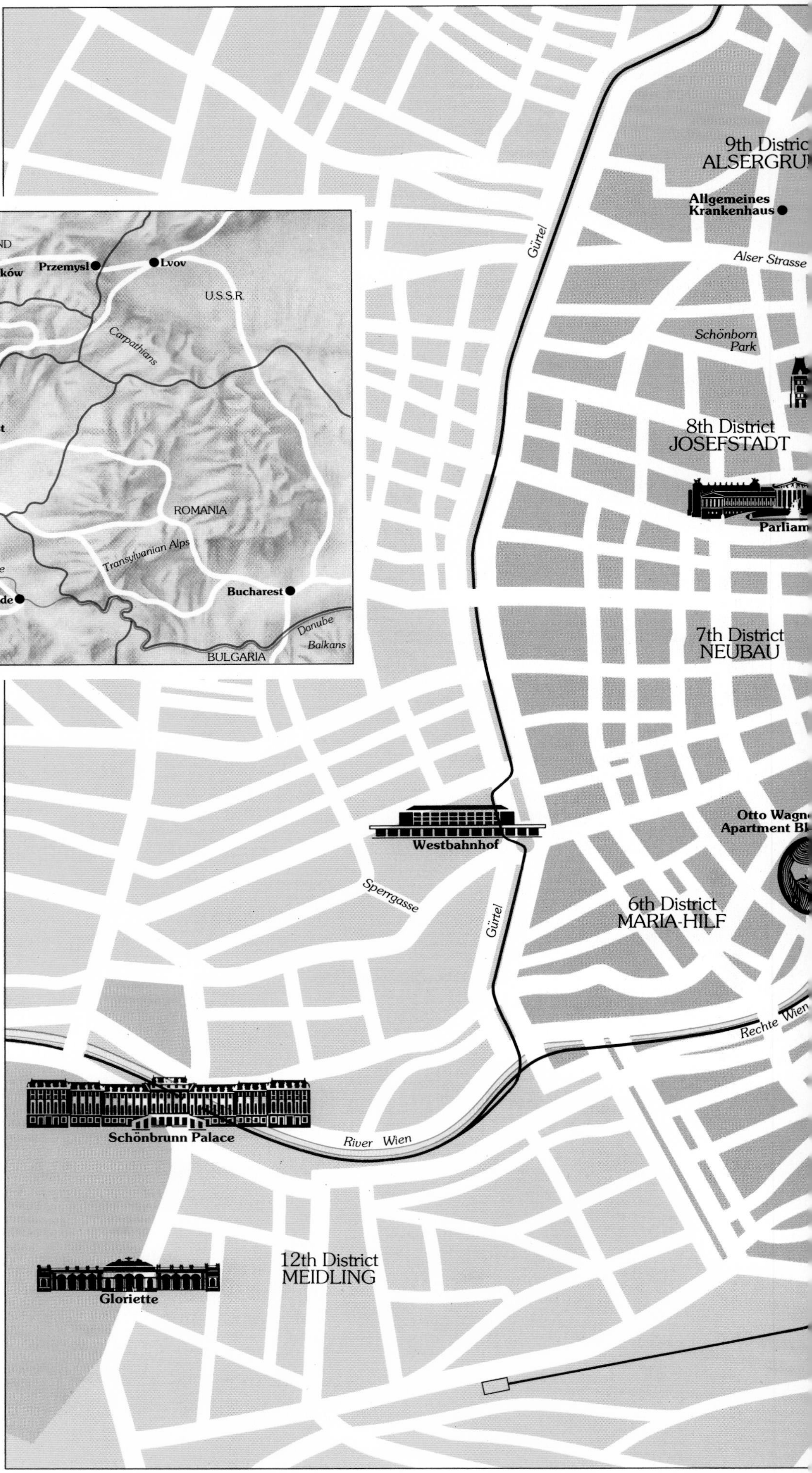

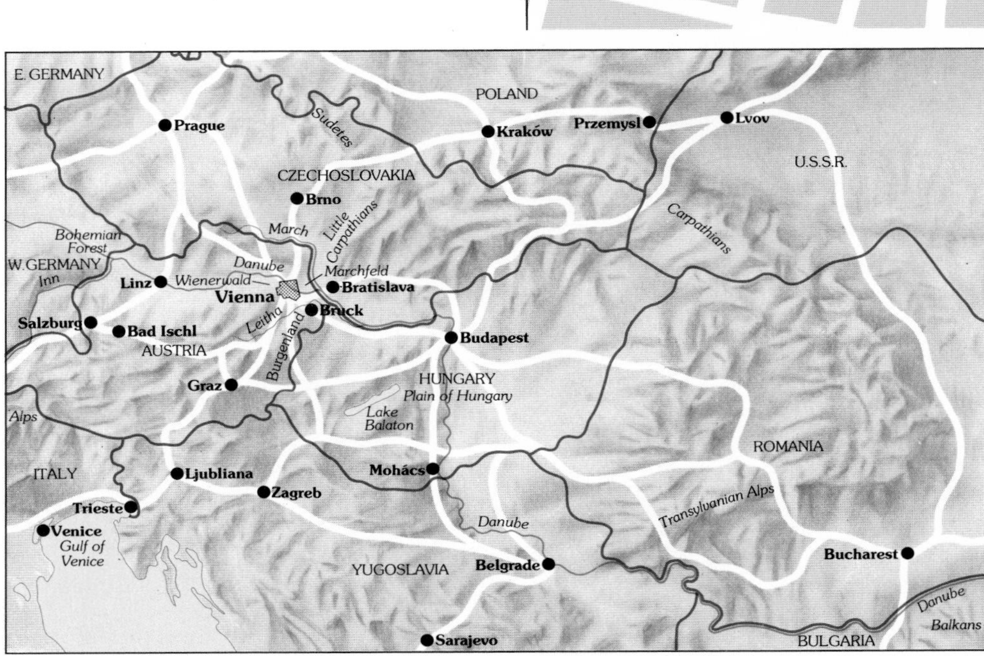

Historic Crossroads

For most of its history Vienna was a fortified stronghold, and its old military boundaries have left their mark. The great 19th-Century encircling boulevard called the Ringstrasse—which follows the line of the town's medieval walls—encloses the area now known as the Inner City (beige on main map, right). An outer line of defences built in the 18th Century has been replaced by a second ring road known as the Gürtel, which now separates the central area (blue) from the suburbs. To the east, the city's defence has always been the Danube. A canalized arm of the river runs through central Vienna, while the main current flows through the outer district of Donaustadt (top right-hand corner).

From the city centre, a web of roads spreads outwards through central Europe (inset map, above). But there is little east-west traffic nowadays. Vienna, once the capital of a vast empire, has become a neutral outpost surrounded on three sides by countries of the East European bloc.

9th Distric
ALSERGRU
Allgemeines Krankenhaus
Gürtel
Alser Strasse
Schönborn Park
8th District
JOSEFSTADT
Parliam
7th District
NEUBAU
Otto Wagn
Apartment Bl
Westbahnhof
Sperrgasse
Gürtel
6th District
MARIA-HILF
Rechte Wien
Schönbrunn Palace
River Wien
12th District
MEIDLING
Gloriette

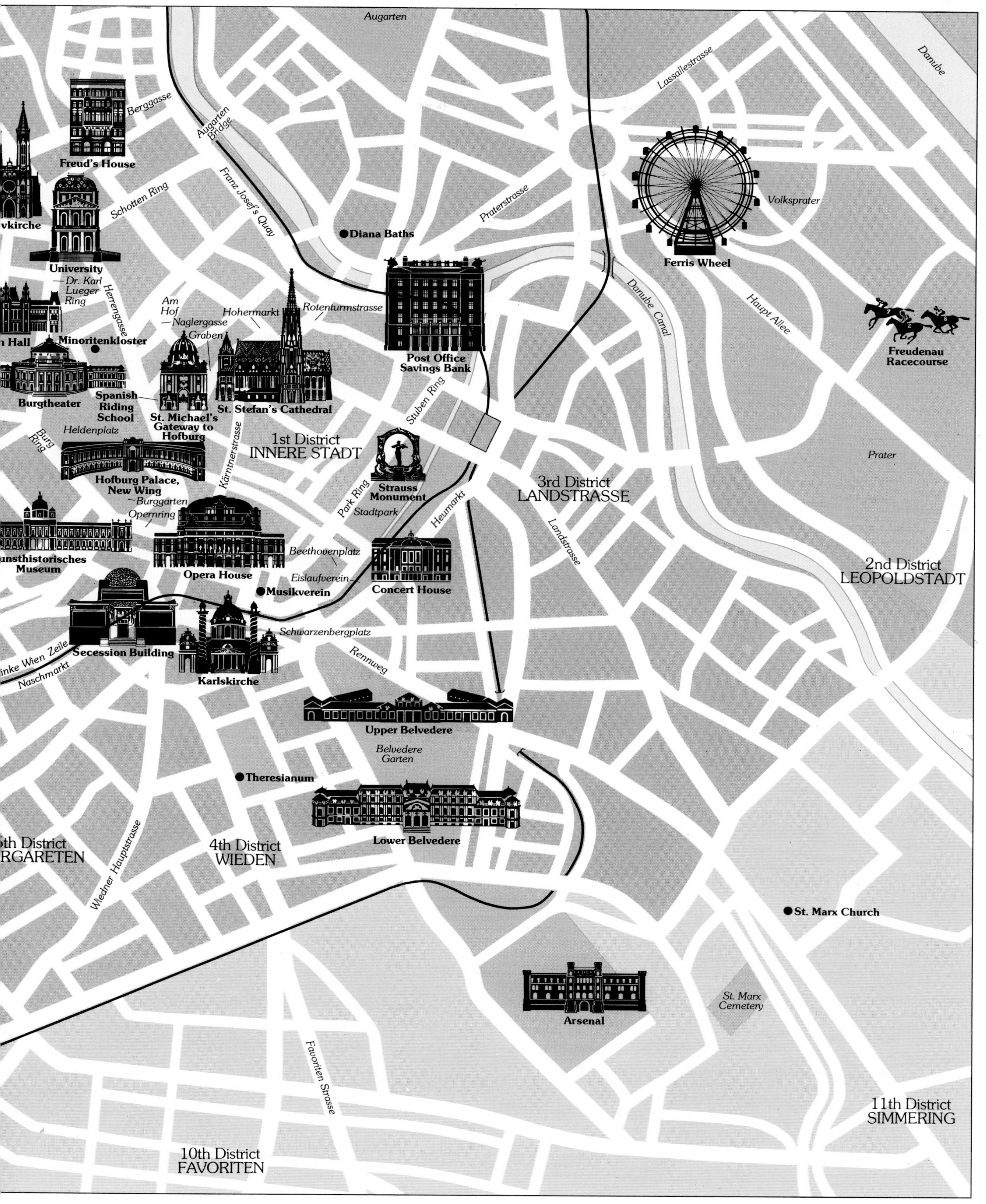
Augarten
Lassallestrasse
Danube
Berggasse
Augarten Bridge
Freud's House
Franz Josef's Quay
Schotten Ring
Praterstrasse
Volksprater
vkirche
Diana Baths
University
Ferris Wheel
Dr. Karl Lueger Ring
Herrengasse
Am Hof
Naglergasse
Hohermarkt
Rotenturmstrasse
Danube Canal
Haupt Allee
Graben
Freudenau Racecourse
h Hall
Minoritenkloster
Post Office Savings Bank
Burgtheater
Spanish Riding School
St. Michael's Gateway to Hofburg
St. Stefan's Cathedral
Stuben Ring
Burg Ring
Heldenplatz
1st District INNERE STADT
Kärntnerstrasse
Prater
Hofburg Palace, New Wing
Strauss Monument
3rd District LANDSTRASSE
Burggarten
Park Ring
Stadtpark
Heumarkt
Opernring
Landstrasse
Beethovenplatz
2nd District LEOPOLDSTADT
unsthistorisches Museum
Opera House
Eislaufverein
Concert House
Musikverein
Schwarzenbergplatz
Rennweg
inke Wien Zeile
Naschmarkt
Secession Building
Karlskirche
Upper Belvedere
Belvedere Garten
Theresianum
Lower Belvedere
th District RGARETEN
4th District WIEDEN
Wiedner Hauptstrasse
St. Marx Church
St. Marx Cemetery
Arsenal
Favoriten Strasse
11th District SIMMERING
10th District FAVORITEN

more patrolling Jeeps, no more zones. By the end of the year, the Viennese newspapers were publishing an unforgettable photograph of the very last Red Army soldier to leave: a major in a trailing greatcoat, with a scowl on his face as he crossed the frontier beyond Bruck to rejoin a military train steaming away into Hungary. Vienna could start up again on its own.

This was unexpected luck. Nobody in the West has yet been able to explain convincingly why the Soviets evacuated their zone with nothing more in return than a guarantee of Austrian neutrality. Stalin was not one to disgorge any morsel he had swallowed, and perhaps it was only his death in 1953 that released Vienna. The quiet sleep of the Viennese is still haunted by the nightmare that they will wake and discover the Red Army once more in possession of the city. I know a writer who lives in a flat right in the centre of Vienna, and not long ago while I was calling on him, a tram outside—a lovely old tram as red and puffy as an archduke—clanged and banged especially loudly. The writer leaped to the window, as pale as could be, saying, "Listen, it's an advance column of Russian tanks!"

And yet, the Viennese are much more resilient than might be imagined. Under pressure, they apparently pump cynicism into their bloodstreams as others do adrenalin. During the last 50 years they have waved goodbye to Habsburgs, Nazis, Soviets. They have learned how to begin from scratch. All the same, the past is a vivid and lively ghost. Whatever can one do with an imperial city that has no empire to back it up? Nobody need mourn, perhaps; but there is no missing the seeping sadness and shrinkage of this city. Like the *Föhn*, or ill-tempered local mind, it is in the climate.

Romantically holding hands, a middle-aged couple wander along an avenue in Schönbrunn Park—laid out in imperial style by the Habsburgs in the 18th Century. On the right, ladies sit gossiping beneath a spectacular array of roses in the Volksgarten, conveniently close to the busy streets of the Inner City.

Vienna's population has dropped from more than two million before the First World War to less than a million and three-quarters. (Over the same period, by contrast, the population of London has risen by one million and that of Paris has remained stable.) Even its preserves of beauty are tinged with defiance, as if to say, you came asking for fun but you'll take away some of the regrets we've felt. All the former corridors of power are under the stringent protection of various fine arts commissions. The balconies of palaces are not used any more for public appearances; they are without function. History here is trauma; everybody has been wounded by it.

It was the spring of 1956 when I returned to Vienna, the first spring of the newly independent city. I arrived at one of the main railway stations, the Westbahnhof, rebuilt—like so much else—in concrete and glass, which can so quickly wipe away the traces of war ruins. The carriages of the continental expresses—there were still Pullman carriages in those days, coloured blue with interiors of polished wood—carried on their sides tin plates announcing their routes, like titles of adventure stories: Vienna-Istanbul, Vienna-Cracow-Smolensk-Moscow, Vienna-Belgrade-Athens.

The air was crisp, its tang indescribable, compounded of freshness, with something extra that was hard to define—what? Brown coal? Rock? The Alps? I knew at once that I was going to feel well, that I would be able to spring out of bed in the morning, with none of that unsatisfied sleepiness of London or Paris. The chestnuts were covered with the pink or white blossoms called *Kerzen*, candles, which can be rhymed most conveniently with *Herzen*, or hearts, in any number of sentimental songs. Lilac, too, was everywhere—boudoir colours and boudoir scent.

I had an address where I was to stay. The home of a Herr Direktor—a businessman—and his wife. I had not met them before, but had an immediate impression of friendliness, as though we had known one another all our lives. His masculine sausage-roll neck and her feminine braided grey hair were to provide me with a setting of home. With them, I knew at once, I could be at ease, so long as nothing too much was asked.

The furniture in the apartment was all of a piece—dark, ornate, unbreakable. On appropriate upholstered surfaces were white or red-headed pins holding the antimacassars in place. Lace curtains blocked off whatever dim light managed to percolate past the shutters, the outer window, the inner window, and the drapes. We moved between the rooms like moles, burrowing along routes designed less for comfort than to present mahogany and teak obstacles. All of it, everything, had survived like this from an earlier generation. It had to do with a way of life, and so it had to be good enough—more than good enough—for the likes of us.

Above the Herr Direktor's apartment, right up under the roof, lived an ancient relation of mine. As an honorary aunt, she was known as Tante Bebe and had proved herself to be as indestructible as Vienna itself. She had got the better of many tiresome things like inflation, bank collapses, the Gestapo. She always wore a black dress, and was small enough and old enough for the word "crone" to fit her perfectly. Her friends were spinsters exactly like her. When one of them went out shopping, say to the grocery store round the corner, another would walk a few yards behind impersonating her maid, and perhaps carrying more than her share of parcels. Few people were taken in by this rather touching charade, but everybody was gratified. I doubt that there could have been more than a few hundred maids in all Vienna at the time, but these elderly ladies were wishfully trying to recreate the world they had lived in with maids galore.

My room was a cavern deep enough to hold a potted palm in one corner and a life-size bronze stork in another, in addition to the usual bed, table and chair and a cupboard as big as a battlement. When the Hungarian Uprising broke out that autumn, three refugees were easily accommodated with me in this same space. The bathroom, on the other hand, was more like an upright coffin. One had to infiltrate it by a sidling movement, ducking to avoid the bulking installation of a wall-mounted water heater whose pipes complained constantly. As for the lavatory, properly known as the *Klo*, it was an object of almost fetishistic attention. Its porcelain bowl had a shallow shelf—the better to examine the true state of one's health, as the Herr Direktor put it; the topic was of inexhaustible interest to the household in general. I could not fail to connect this typically Viennese concern with Freud's more intimate theories of creativity and evacuation—theories which no doubt Freud had elaborated because he was Viennese.

A tram rumbles round a curve of Ottakringer Strasse in Vienna's 16th District—a village until swallowed up by the expanding city in the late 19th Century.

At meal times, the fixed compass-points of the day, we would foregather and politely inquire of one another about the latest development in our lives—intellectual, financial, bodily. So much could apparently happen in just a few hours. Nothing was too trivial to discuss or analyse from every angle. The Herr Direktor was appalled, I think, to discover that, although I knew Latin and Greek and could give some account of, say, Italian painting, double-entry book-keeping was a closed art to me, and that I was glad about it. Clearly I was doomed to be a dilettante, a type he and his friends in Vienna despised because there were such multitudes of them. Nevertheless, he took me in hand, and much of the lore I have about Vienna stems from his instruction.

For instance, he showed me where a Gestapo interrogation centre had been (could the street really have been called the Mozartgasse?). He explained how the Soviets had taken over this centre for their own secret police, the NKVD. The cracks in the pavement, he said, had been made by poor devils preferring to leap to their deaths from some upper floor rather than face the torments reserved for them inside. He indicated where a Rothschild palace had been pulled down to make room for trade union offices, and recounted the history of the street then known as Lassallestrasse, after a 19th-Century socialist: it had started out as the Crown Prince Rudolf Strasse and, during the course of its existence, had also been called the Reichsbrückenstrasse and, he recollected, the Red Army Bridge Avenue.

The Herr Direktor had his *Stammtisch*, or favourite table, in a café; there he regularly met his circle of friends, few of whom ever came to the apartment. Through one of them it was arranged for me to attend some lectures at the university, where it was felt I could best improve my German. Dreary, dusty hours of pedagogy followed. It was a claustrophobic atmosphere that had hardly survived elsewhere in Europe; I found that in Vienna learning was a thing apart, performed for its own sake, not in order to enrich life. *Maturas*, or school-leaving certificates, were stepping-stones; doctorates were worth their weight in good solid money. Professors, one felt, might well cuff one about the ears—and they would certainly blight a career if they did not care for the careerist.

To the dismay of the Herr Direktor, I took to dropping out of this stifling atmosphere, preferring to hang about all day with other students who were also thoroughly fed up but not prepared to do anything about it. The group was known as "The Chair-Seat Polishers", a typically Viennese expression; but all of them, as far as I know, became proficient and respectable lawyers, accountants and businessmen, just like their fathers before them. Wild oats in Vienna are a pretty light crop, and hardly last a season. Through my association with "The Chair-Seat Polishers" I learnt a great deal more German than I would have done at the university. Or to be more accurate, I began to master the familiarities of the

In one of the mouldering courtyards of a mid-19th-Century block of flats in the Burggasse district, a mother and child have thrown open a ground-floor window for some fresh air. The Viennese call this kind of building a Durchhaus —literally a "through house"—because the successive interior courtyards are connected to the streets by gloomy passage-ways.

Viennese dialect called *Wienerisch*. In Vienna everybody talks this broadly accented and friendly relation of German. It is a closed shop for those who speak it, far more so than Cockney in London or *argot* in Paris. It is social cement and brings the most diverse people into the same club.

Wienerisch has a big vocabulary, a regional mish-mash incorporating German tidbits, Slav borrowings, Yiddish, Italian—anything handy, really. Much of *Wienerisch* is subtly denigrating; the Viennese delight in humourously putting down people and values, or in drawing parallels far-fetched enough to raise a smile—like calling vanilla sauce "canary's milk". All with-it speech, like *Wienerisch*, has an onomatopoeic element. What could be more expressive of a call-girl than *Flitscherl*, or of the police than *Höh* ("them at the top")?

For the sake of all-togetherness, first names are dispensed with. Either a person is addressed in the third person with the utmost formality, or else a friendly abbreviation is found: Bigi, Gigi, Guggi, Bichi, Coci, Fifi, Desi, Tesi, Gusti, Poldi, Litzi, Mitzi, Lulu, Wuwu, Lolo, Kiki, Niki, Riki are some of the most common. Just as important is the diminution of words, which renders them affectionate and familiar: for instance, a love affair is a *Pantscherl*—the syllables themselves giving the game away. The ending *-erl* can be applied to any noun to reduce its impact, as when the telephone operator warns of a long wait before a connection can be made with the words, *"nur a kleines Momenterl, bitte"*. Any amount of irony can be adduced by means of this suffix, as the Austrian playwright Johann Nestroy demonstrated while the 1848 radical upheavals were in the air, by having his characters talk of *Revolution-erl, Konstitution-erl, Parlament-erl.*

Of Viennese words that have made their way round the world, *Waltz* is the best example, but there are also *Schmalz* (some authorities dissent, because of the Yiddish derivations) and *Strudel* and *Schnitzel*. A few words which have not travelled ought nevertheless to be singled out. *Schmäh* is an original Viennese concept of self-salesmanship; ingratiating oneself through flattery or cleverness for the sake of some ulterior purpose. *Schlamperei* means dirtiness combined with ineffectiveness, or getting things wrong; it was used in a celebrated context by the socialist Viktor Adler, who described the Habsburg Empire as "despotism tempered by *Schlamperei*". *Gemütlich*, much used in Vienna, says all there is to be said about being cosy. Indeed, words of this sort convey more about Vienna than any number of books.

Much has changed since those post-war years when I first got to know Vienna and *Wienerisch*. Thinking back, I sometimes wonder whether my memories are not just literary imaginings, for the scarred austerity of that period is well concealed nowadays by the consumer society. Affluence has come with a vengeance. The autobahns into the city are chock-a-block. Rush-hour is a nightmare, far removed from the time I remember when traffic policemen recognized every single driver because there were so few, and the drivers responded by leaving a Christmas present of a bottle or two of wine at those intersections where they were most warmly saluted.

Machine tools, heavy industry, textiles, banks—all are tied in today with the German economy and benefit from its strength. Agriculture, timber and water for hydro-electricity are the basis of the economy, to which must be added the discovery of oil, not many miles north of Vienna, in quantities sufficient to satisfy nearly a third of the country's energy needs. No less a person than Hermann Goering took an interest in exploiting these resources, but the huge petro-chemical complex just outside Vienna has come into its own only in the last 15 years.

Since the war Vienna has blandly refurbished itself, brushing up its past for the visitors of the present. The hotel business is booming. Thousands of bedrooms, their cubic footage tightly regulated, have been provided for the tourists who bring with them so high a percentage of the hard-currency earnings. The Viennese have begun to lay it on thick. When the continental expresses stop here, they are met by station-masters in smarter kit than anywhere else along the line, and receptionists at Schwechat Airport wear folk costume on special occasions. The Viennese revival is a miracle and, like the best of miracles, also a matter for self-congratulation. Prosperity fits everyone well. Faces in shops, offices and factories are eagerly commercial, not bored. Leisure, too, has flowed back. Most people come to work early, at eight in the morning or sooner, but they feel justified in knocking off early, probably at four in the afternoon.

Driving into Vienna, from whichever direction, you could well overlook

At the entrance to a block of flats in the Neubau district, a Hausbesorger, or caretaker, glances up through the glass door of his office. The Hausbesorger keeps a sharp eye on tenants and their guests, making sure that none of the house rules and regulations is infringed.

A pensioner on the landing of one of Vienna's Bassena-Wohnungen—or "basin flats"—prepares to draw water from the cast-iron fixture that has given such buildings their name. Tenants of these 19th-Century blocks have to share the single basin provided for each floor.

the miracle. Thousands of blocks of flats put up before the First World War look as though they may have been running down ever since. Some, which were at the top end of the social scale, are enormous rabbit-warrens with perhaps a hundred or more families living in them. They have several interior courtyards, a little mildewy, the outer plaster streaked with greenish stains. Doors and stairways lead off the courtyards. Directions for finding an address in such a house ought to be given carefully, to save a long wandering through stony hallways and passages, deserted but for the echo of footsteps.

Lower down the scale are residential streets stretching like ravines, the façades of the houses as grimy and hard as a rockface. A century of brown coal-dust, dug in Bohemia or Moravia and burned in boilers built in cellars like ships' holds, has settled on them, although the dirty effect belies the solid craftsmanship of the stone. Most of these houses have five storeys, three flats to a storey, and they are known as *Bassena-Wohnungen*, after the *Bassena*, or basin and cold-water tap that was an original wall fixture on each of the central landings. Before modern plumbing was put in, everybody had to fetch water for household purposes from these taps. Five-litre jugs were designed to fit exactly into the *Bassena*; they are now sought after in antique shops. Next to the *Bassena* on the landing was a lavatory, again communal, and that completed the original plumbing installations. A bath was out of the question.

Since the war a whole industry has grown up to make good the lack of modern conveniences in the *Bassena-Wohnungen*. All over Vienna a million cupboards, nooks and corners, parts of staircases, angles of rooms and storage areas, broom spaces, falsely partitioned lobbies, and heaven-knows-what unexpected crannies have been converted into showers or bathrooms. Some are so minute that it is impossible to stand upright in them; others are mad inventors' arrangements that fold up against the wall by rope and pulley. Hip baths have come into their own in all shapes and sizes, often suitable only for yoga improvisations.

The trouble with *Bassena-Wohnungen* when they were built was less their discomfort and lack of amenities than the rigid pattern of life they imposed. The urban poor lived exactly alike, compressed into a housing grid without nuances. Just to see the outside of such a tenement is to be able to predict correctly the interiors, the lay-out, the position of every kitchen window, the height of each ceiling, and the single life-style permissible in such surroundings.

To make sure of absolute conformity, the rules and regulations concerning dogs, carpet-beating, noise, gardening and so forth were pinned up in each and every entrance, and they are still to be seen today. These rules were enforced by a guardian who was installed by the building's owner in a rent-free flat, or if not by a guardian then a *concierge*, also known as *Hausmeister, Hausbesorger*, or *Portier*. Once such a person was a stock

The Karl Marx Hof, appropriately reddish in colour, stretches for more than half a mile along the Heiligenstädter Strasse in the district of Döbling. Built in 1930 by the town council, or Gemeinde, it housed 1,300 workers' families and was a showpiece of the former Habsburg capital, known as "Red Vienna" because of its conversion to socialism.

character in the city; a source of myth and legend, Cerberus and slut, possessor of majestic bunches of keys. The *concierges* inhabited rooms with a special smell of hydrogen sulphide and goulash and garlic and pets, and their manners were mocked.

Viennese *concierges* are a dying race, no longer the centre of gossip; but whether in charge of *Bassena-Wohnungen* or a palace, they still perform their one universal ceremony of locking the main doors of the buildings at half-past-nine or ten at night. If you happen to be out without a key, that's that. If you happen to be a guest inside, then your host must traipse down with his key to let you out. The atmosphere of doing something furtive is enhanced because the light on the landing is operated by an automatic switch that allows only a minute's worth of electricity at a time. Much groping in the dark follows.

Here and there through the outer approaches of the city are the mammoth constructions of officialdom, the proletarian housing blocks constructed by the Gemeinde Wien, the socialist City Hall administration. They obstruct every view, and would be immediately recognizable even if each one did not proudly proclaim exactly what it is: its name, year of construction and so on, appear in tall red lettering on one side of the building. Almost half of Vienna lives in one of these Gemeinde buildings, and half of Vienna is therefore conscious of its dependence on bureaucratic grace and favour. The majority of these buildings are several storeys higher than the rest of the city, and therefore out of scale, self-assertive. They are finished in unworked cement, rough cast, and cover the entire range of beiges and greys. Just occasionally one wall has been brightened with a fresco—some work officially commissioned to cheer people up, perhaps depicting a jolly harvest scene or an abstract design.

If you do not cling fast to the idea that this is deliberately cheap and subsidized housing to improve the living conditions of the masses (and has something to do with winning elections), you may well dislike Vienna from the outset. Since the 1920s, the Gemeinde has set the tone of Vienna, and it is not a tone that cares to please. On the contrary, the drabness and aggression are deliberate. In those early days after the departure of the Habsburgs, the Gemeinde wished to express the power of the working class, and maybe even to put a good measure of class fear into everybody else. The blanker the walls, the more secure the class bastions. No frills, no window casements, no unnecessary expense. Above all, no possible excuse for the dreaded label of "bourgeois".

Nearing the centre of Vienna you notice countervailing pockets of something quite different. First a glimpse of a tiled mansard roof, visible just above a wall, with a central gate, a grille, stone supports, suggestions of courtyards, or of a farm engulfed by the town. Then come perhaps two or three houses, or maybe a whole terrace, fronting a canal or the embankments of the River Wien. Their façades are painted with that

Vienna was in its heyday as capital of the Austro-Hungarian Empire when this panoramic lithograph, viewing the city from the south-west, was published in 1873. In the foreground, the Schwarzenberg Palace (centre) with its squat circular tower is flanked by the domed Karlskirche (left) and the long façade of the Lower Belvedere Palace (right). Behind these landmarks, the gardens and avenues of the recently completed Ringstrasse loop the Inner City, ending in bridges over the Danube Canal which crosses the picture in the middle distance.

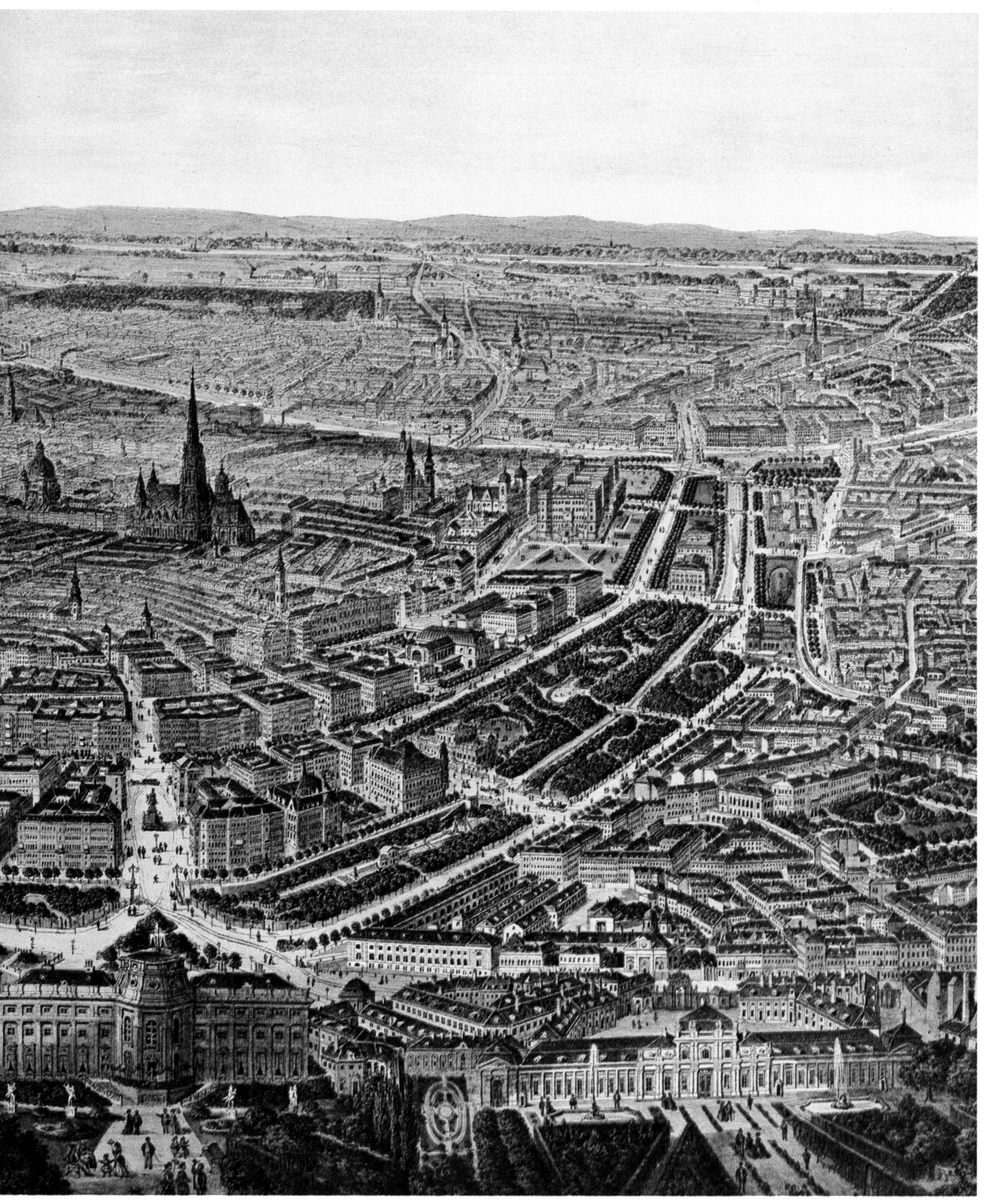

wonderful distressed yellow or ochre wash, the historic colour of this part of the world. The predominant yellow will be set off by matching washes in greens and soft pinks and white and even duck-egg blue. This is Vienna as we know it from Mozart—importunate, irrepressible under the weight of everything, including the Gemeinde, winking its survival or at least its refusal to be part of the crowd.

Frivolity is the tone here. Window casements are adorned with baroque or rococo fluting, swags, central scallops, carved bunches of flowers, musical instruments on a plaque, or lines as swift as the swing of a branch of a tree. There are flattened Ionic columns, capitals, small round *oeil-de-boeuf* windows, plasterwork in available spaces, ironwork for fun. Much of this is dilapidated, to be sure, like a kind of open-air antique shop, dreadfully neglected and run-down, suggesting that everything has been left to moulder in the absence of customers. But over the last 20 years there has been a flurry of preservation—new roofs, structural repairs, licks of paint. The Gemeinde style does not have it all its own way. Pleasure for its own non-utilitarian sake is hard to kill.

Closing in, you are bound at last to connect with the Ring. Few capitals in Europe, I suppose, have so well-known a piece of 19th-Century town-scaping, out-Haussmanning what the Baron Georges Haussmann did for the Paris of Napoleon III. As its name indicates, the Ring is simply the circumference of the Inner City. Not much more than two miles round, it can be walked quite easily. The Ring was begun on the initiative of the Emperor Franz Josef and was created in the boom years after 1857, the period known as the *Gründerzeit*. It was a symbolic gesture, for the fortifications of the medieval walled city were erased to make way for it. In a sense, Vienna was thrown open to the industrial age, for the city could hardly have expanded and developed otherwise.

For 30 years, the Ring was under construction, an experimental paradise. Critics have argued that it was a weakness of the period not to have an overriding or uniform architectural style. Certainly what went up is pastiche, even parody. Each stretch of garden or open space leads to another sample of something outlandish, imitative. The University is early Tuscan Renaissance in style and the *Rathaus*, or Town Hall, is flamboyant 19th-Century Gothic. The Votivkirche with its distinctive twin church spires is also mock-Gothic, put up to celebrate Franz Josef's escape from a Hungarian tailor who pulled a knife on him. The parliament building is pure wish-fulfilment, a Grecian heaven-knows-what with columns and peristyles suggesting the ideals of Periclean Athens (which were otherwise not much to be found in this particular empire). Statues of thinkers and would-be democrats, for some reason mostly in the nude and holding a rampant horse by the mane, strike wonderfully idealized poses on every side, with plenty of gilt and verdigris in the background.

The only building on the Ring that was seriously damaged in the Second

World War was the Opera House, whose original architect had committed suicide when Franz Josef permitted himself some perfectly reasonable observations on its dubious perspectives. The gilded auditorium and the vast stage were bombed and gutted by fire in 1945, but the shell of the building survived and the interior was soon rebuilt and restored to a condition so closely resembling the original that few people could notice the difference. On the practical side, the number of seats had been reduced for the sake of better viewing, and the stage machinery had been modernized. After an interval of 10 years, the house re-opened with a performance of Beethoven's *Fidelio*, an opera whose première was staged in Vienna in 1805.

In the hundred years since its creation, the Ring has mellowed. Absurd it may be, stranded like Noah's Ark in the flood-tide of the 20th Century, but it is lovable for all that—perhaps because of all that. Double avenues of linden and chesnut and plane trees have grown around it, shading the trams rumbling past on the cobblestones and hiding the airline offices and neon-lit company headquarters that keep it alive.

The Ring is a demarcation; it is where passports to the mythical Vienna of the mind must be presented. Within it, the Inner City is all history, and history within walking distance. The agreeable little streets were obviously intended for the concourse of citizens, never for motor cars. At the nub sits the Hofburg, the sprawling imperial palace where Franz Josef lived out his reign, ruling his empire as all his family had done before him. And all around, within the shortest of carriage drives, are the palaces of the great families who arrived from every province of the empire—Hungary, Italy, Bohemia, Moravia, the German lands—to get their hands upon the levers of patronage and power. These palaces are heaped together, making do with the smallest plots, constricted, sharing party walls; but their façades are in fine display, designed to be seen at a squint upwards or sideways instead of across open grass or a forecourt.

Sometimes only a plaque in white enamel decorated with the red and white flags of Austria, reveals that some building was a palace. Caprara, Esterházy, Pallavicini, Porcia, Mollard, Trautson, Schoenborn, Kinsky—the great imperial names are commemorated by mere signposts for tourists. Inside, there is likely to be a ministry, an import-export business, a consulate, a restaurant. Even the carriage entrance of the great Belvedere Palace, built for Prince Eugene of Savoy in the early 18th Century, has lettering proclaiming that here is the headquarters of some firm of international hauliers. How are the mighty fallen. Starting to sense that, and to question it, you have arrived.

The Extravagant Imperial Style

Seen from under a canopy of horse-chestnut leaves, the Parliament building along the Ringstrasse lifts a rooftop row of statues against the evening sky.

For size, scope and architectural diversity, few public works programmes have ever matched Vienna's Ringstrasse, the two-and-a-half-mile horseshoe of grandiose buildings and tree-lined avenues that loops the old town centre. The project was the brainchild of the Emperor Franz Josef, who made room for it in 1857 by ordering the demolition of the city's medieval fortifications. In their place, over the next 30 years, rose churches, palaces, museums, government buildings and apartment blocks—the whole array designed in a mish-mash of exhumed styles from neo-Gothic to fake Renaissance. Encrusted with statues and lined with echoing expanses of marble, the buildings on the Ringstrasse seem the product of an appetite for grandeur run wild—as though Vienna could already sense that the days of imperial glory were numbered.

A mass of statues and trophies, including a pair of classical tunics above the pediment, decorate the Neue Burg Palace.

Symbols of imperial power—among them fasces, swords and standards—frame windows of Franz Josef's War Ministry.

The Town Hall's 320-foot neo-Gothic spire intrudes on the decorum of its neighbours, a row of once-private mansions built in a self-consciously noble style.

A row of grave-faced caryatids lines a gallery in the Palace of Justice. Ringstrasse architects liked to elaborate their interiors as much as their façades.

A 10-foot-high marble statue of Justice looks down the staircase of the palace's central hall, reducing a passing lawyer to insignificance.

Holding a Winged Victory in her hand, a huge statue of Pallas Athene—goddess of wisdom—stands to attention before the Parliament building's Austrian flag.

The goddess and her attendant—popular subjects for mythologizing artists—reappear in mosaic over a fountain in the Stubenring section of the Ringstrasse.

Amid the red-and-white Austrian flags on the rooftop of the Parliament building, a crazy jumble of marble and bronze statues creates mythological confusion.

2
The Storybook Empire

Consigned to an obscure storage vault in the Hofburg Palace, a plaster bust of the Emperor Franz Josef stares indomitably into the darkness. Having held the Austrian Empire together for 68 years, the Emperor died in 1916, two years before its collapse.

The Alps, Europe's great spinal feature, are a splendid redoubt, barricading Mediterraneans from northerners, olives from pines—and where they stop in the east is Vienna. There, the huge peaks that straddle France, Italy, Germany, Switzerland and Austria diminish into foothills—the cosy hillocks of the Wienerwald, or Vienna Woods. Nature becomes domesticated. These much-celebrated woods of beech and fir spread behind the city in a protective crescent from the north-west to the south-west, and some of the hills—the Kahlenberg, the Leopoldsberg, the Cobenzl—are ideal vantage points for surveying Vienna and its surroundings.

Over the last hundred years, houses have been built on the upper slopes of the hills, although the vineyards lower down have remained as they always were. Roads and neat trails looping about in the Wienerwald lead to cafés and restaurants and open-air terraces, a few of them converted from former hunting-lodges of the imperial family, but all designed for stylized excursions. Through the woods come couples keen to look like their grandparents, male and female wearing wool socks and climbing boots, leather-shorted or knickerbockered, walking sticks or *Alpenstock* in hand, green hats on their heads. If they want to do the thing properly, they will leave the car at home and walk up from the tram terminal at the city limits, and after a whopping meal they will walk back.

These Wienerwald hills are a thousand or so feet above the city. From the Leopoldsberg, which has one of the best views, you can see the well-known landmarks of Habsburg Vienna. First of all, there is the spire of St. Stefan's Cathedral, dating from the 13th Century and familiarly known to the Viennese as "Old Steffel". Then the Ring can be made out—the public buildings on it and the verdigris domes of 18th-Century churches. Today, the city covers 150 square miles, a third more than when the last Habsburg emperor left, and the aerial perspectives take in factories and tall chimneys and new bridges spreading outwards. The most striking element in the panorama below is the Danube. Seen from the Wienerwald hills, the river is an evanescent ribbon that gleams brown and tawny, sometimes silver with the light full on it—but never in anyone's true experience, come rain or sun or snow, blue. To call it "The Blue Danube" was a stroke of romantic inspiration on the part of the Viennese composer Johann Strauss; and fair enough, because there is something of the romantic spirit in the meeting of the Alps and the Danube.

The river has gathered pace and stature since leaving its obscure source in West Germany, near the town of Donaueschingen. Vienna is the first capital on its way, with Budapest and Belgrade to follow before the Danube debouches into its vast delta of reed-beds and waterways on the Romanian shores of the Black Sea. At Vienna, the river is strong and sinuous, although it has been like that only since the middle of the last century, when it was canalized to prevent flooding. Before then it spilled through several courses, creating marshlands.

A marshy landscape, known as the Lobau, still exists on the outskirts of the city, and sometimes during an unseasonal winter these floodlands freeze over and become an open-air skating rink. I was there one January when that happened, and people took their children out on cross-country skating expeditions—something the children would one day be telling their children about. The Lobau is a moody and desolate expanse of flatlands, straggly with weeds and willows, a place where the wild duck take flight in the evening. A famous popular song has a refrain "Down in the Lobau once I kissed a girl", commemorating its waterside haunts. It seems doomed to disappear under increasing urban clutter: the television towers and satellite-tracking stations, motorways and slabbed concrete buildings which cities dump at their edges.

Paradoxically, the best way to see the Danube is to be at a distance from it, on top of a hill in the Wienerwald. In the city, thanks to the tidy courses through which it flows, the Danube is missing, and missed. From above, its influence is obvious. Trade between east and west has taken this route for as long as history has been recorded; the Danube was *the* alternative to the Mediterranean shipping lanes, *the* way of circumventing the Alps for traffic between northern Europe and the Levant. Here, nestled against the mountains, was a natural site for a community that could make a living on the trade passing up and down the river.

The first settlement of any size on this site was called Vindobona, meaning White Field. It was founded in the 4th Century B.C. by Celts, and became a Roman fortified town in the First Century A.D. Up there at the end of the Alps, the Romans must have felt lost to the civilized world, though with the mountains behind them they at least had the reassurance that nobody could storm them from the rear. Otherwise the place was open. To the east, in a great semi-circle to the horizon, is the sweep of a plain known as the Marchfeld, a name associated with battles immemorial. The Marchfeld stretches out to the great Hungarian plain and on to the Carpathians and to Asia; and from it have poured the conquering hordes of Avars, Huns, Magyars—nomad tribesmen who rode without stirrups and plundered or burned everything in sight. The Marchfeld has been like a carpet for invaders to walk over. It is the natural approach to the Alps and then, along the Danube, to the heart of Western Europe. Sometimes invaders came the other way—for instance, the early Germans who settled Austria. Napoleon Bonaparte, too, followed this path eastwards to seize Vienna, and so did Adolf Hitler.

Below the Vienna Woods, the Danube skirts Vienna's eastern districts, dominated by a television tower and the United Nations complex (centre).

Across this plain, holding more or less to the Danube, ran the *limes*, the limit of the Roman Empire. This was the boundary of the far-flung province of Pannonia, covering much the same area as present-day Austria. Fortresses were strung along the frontier, and their scattered ruins can still be seen. In a field near the village of Rohrau, a day's forced march east of Vienna, stands a solitary and majestic Roman arch—virtually all that is left standing of the fortress town of Carnuntum. In their time the Roman watchmen and sentries had looked past it, waiting for barbarians who one day were going to drive them back for good.

Ten miles beyond ancient Carnuntum, barely 30 miles from Vienna, lies the frontier of the Socialist Republic of Czechoslovakia. Those 30 miles from Vienna are a short span on the ground but a huge divide in the facts of everyday life. To the Viennese, driving down country roads and gaping across the frontier is quite as conventional a Sunday outing as a session in a café in the Vienna Woods. Deep in the Viennese psyche lies the thought that Czechoslovakia still is Bohemia, a province of the Habsburg Empire, and that its inhabitants are Bemmen, that slightly down-putting Viennese expression for all Czechs and Slovaks, whether from Bohemia or not. Bohemians rich and poor used to flock into the imperial capital, and to this day Vienna has a larger Czech population than any city except Prague.

Arriving by road from Vienna, you reach the Czechoslovak frontier where it runs along the Danube. On the north side of the river, beyond high bluffs, stands the city of Bratislava, or Pressburg to Germans. The Austrian writer Franz Kafka once described how the journey between Vienna and Bratislava took half a day by ordinary town tram, and how odd it was to travel in this way through cornfields with poppies. At the border bridge, Slovak guards, armed and bored, stand about as though waiting to perform parts in a bad movie. Little traffic comes through, except perhaps a van on some mysterious errand, and then the guards laconically swing up the barrier for it. Tourists, of course, are thoroughly searched. The smallest false move here, one sees, will end in tragedy.

About the same distance south of Vienna is the border of the People's Republic of Hungary. To get there, you pass through the Austrian province of the Burgenland, a kind of no-man's land, very Catholic, with numerous Croat inhabitants. The farm buildings are one storey high and stand around an inner yard which can be shut by a heavy door large enough for a hay-wagon. Storks nest upon the chimney-pots. Customs, traditions, courtesies seem in fine fettle. But beyond the picturesque villages of Rust, St. Margarethen, Andau, there are signposts with skulls and crossbones, warning that the frontier with Hungary is close. Suddenly one meets barbed wire, a long ploughed strip of open ground, and electronic sensors to detect any movement. In watch-towers, at regular intervals, Hungarian sentries in pairs search the countryside through

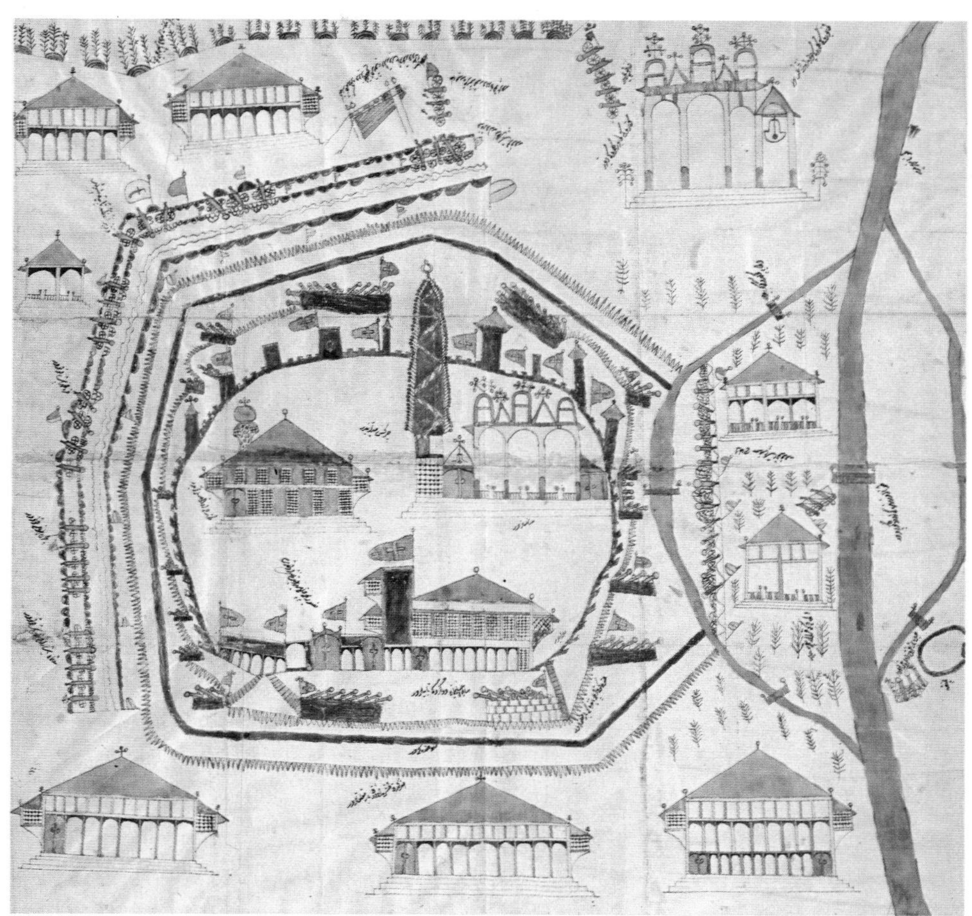

A Turkish map of Vienna, drawn during the 1683 Ottoman siege, provides details of the city's defences—battlemented walls with towers at intervals, a ring of cannon emplacements, a wide ditch (solid brown line) and an outer slope bristling with iron spikes. The Turks were soundly beaten when the Habsburgs' Christian allies arrived. By the end of the 17th Century they had been driven out of Central Europe.

field-glasses. Nothing stirs at the Iron Curtain, which reaches to the Baltic in one direction and to the Black Sea in the other.

The rival tensions of Europe meet, here, at Vienna's backdoor, as they did so often in the past. The Soviets have stopped virtually on the old *limes* of the Romans. Where they and their satellites now look in, the Romans once looked out. History seems to enjoy these sinister jokes.

In the end, there was no holding the line the Romans had drawn in this wilderness. During the barbarian invasions of the 5th Century A.D., the province of Pannonia became a territory to be fought over by all-comers. The Dark Ages descended. Eventually Vindobona emerged with new fortifications, a new name—Wenia, precursor of Vienna—and a new importance given it by the feudal landowners who rose to power in this part of Central Europe: the Babenbergs of Austria and later the Przemysls of Bohemia. Virtually no monuments remain from that period, and its history is vague. The thousandth birthday of Austria was celebrated in 1976, a year as well chosen as any. But the date to remember is 1278, when a Count Rudolf Habsburg, already elected King of Germany, defeated Ottokar Przemysl at the battle of the Marchfeld and took possession of Vienna and the Austrian lands for his family. The Habs-

Viewed across the River Wien and the greenery of the Stadtpark, the copper dome of the Karlskirche—modelled on the cupola of St. Peter's in Rome—swells above the city's roofs. The church—one of the most adventurous examples of the baroque style that swept Vienna in the 18th Century—was designed by Johann Fischer von Erlach and includes such theatrical features as a pair of minaret-like pillars (here floodlit at dusk) and squat side towers whose roofs are designed on the curviform lines of a Chinese tea-house.

burgs already owned land in Alsace and Switzerland, small territories round which their Central European empire was to be constructed. They were to be synonymous with Vienna for six and a half centuries, an achievement of stability and power unmatched in these unruly parts of Europe.

The historians' favourite quotation about the Habsburgs is a line of Latin verse: *"Bella gerant alii; tu, felix Austria, nube* (Others may conduct wars, but you, happy Austria, should conduct marriages)." Through marriage, the empire was carefully constructed. The first two centuries following Count Rudolf's accession had produced nothing but petty warfare among the princely families of Central Europe. Then, in 1477, Maximilian of Habsburg married Mary, daughter of Charles the Bold, Duke of Burgundy. Charles the Bold had been killed in battle against the French a few weeks before the marriage, so Maximilian inherited all the Duke's lands. Burgundy, which included the rich lowlands of Flanders, was one of the strongest and best organized states in Europe; it had no real connection with Austria, not even a geographical one, but Burgundian wealth helped to secure the Habsburgs and enabled them to embark on a campaign of military aggrandizement. Their local duchy was soon transformed into a European power.

The next generation of Habsburgs pursued the same policy. Maximilian's son Philip married Joanna, heiress to the Spanish throne, so that Maximilian's grandson, the great Charles V, inherited Spain and all its possessions, including the colonies in the New World. In the 16th Century, the yellow and black standard of the Habsburgs, with its double-headed eagle, flew over a greater territory than any other in the world, and it was never quite to lose its prestige. Even after the fall of the Habsburgs in 1918, its appeal remained so powerful that the standard had to be outlawed by the Republic; today, anyone who wants to fly it for a pageant or a film has to seek permission from the government.

Charles V ceded the German and Slav provinces of his empire to his younger brother Ferdinand I. Just as Rome and Constantinople had been twin capitals of the Roman Empire, so both Madrid and Vienna were seats of Habsburg administration, at first complementary, gradually diverging. Ferdinand had been brought up in Spain, and when he established himself in Vienna, several leading Spanish families had joined his court. The influence of Spain on Vienna survived to some extent. A few Spanish families, like the Counts Hoyos, remained in the city, and so did some of the official family portraits by Velazquez (now kept in the Kunsthistorisches Museum), showing that heavy and increasingly prominent lower lip that became a characteristic of the Spanish branch. Spanish etiquette prevailed at court, and vestiges of it can still be seen today. In the showpiece dining-room of the Hofburg Palace, the knives, forks and spoons are laid out Spanish-style, to the right of the place at table—a perfect small tease for the tourists. Best known of these historic

Vienna's Ruling Sign

Ever since the 12th Century, an eagle with outstretched wings has been the heraldic emblem of Vienna and its rulers, and images of the fierce bird can be seen all over the city. Most depict the double-headed eagle of the Habsburg family, the *Doppeladler*, which gazes out symbolically to the eastern and western reaches of the Habsburg Empire.

One such royal emblem looms in black stone over the Beethovenplatz, clutching an orb and sceptre (top row, centre); another one, gilded, decorates a concert hall, the Musikverein (middle row, rear right), while a gathering of wrought-iron eagles creates a splendid grille above a doorway on the Ringstrasse (bottom row, near right). The Habsburg device also found its way on to more utilitarian objects, such as a cocoa tin (bottom row, far right) from Demel, confectioners to the court of the Emperor Franz Josef, and an 18th-Century inn sign (top row, rear right).

After the dismemberment of the Habsburg dominions in 1919, one of the imperial eagle's heads was axed by government decree. A bronze apotheosis of the Austrian Republic's single-headed emblem rises above Parliament (top row, far right); its talons clutch a hammer and sickle—representing industrial and farm workers—and dangle broken chains, which symbolize the winning of freedom from Nazi rule in 1945. Elsewhere, the single-headed eagle glares from the registration plate of an official's car (middle row, second left) and spreads vast wings across the magnificent tiled roof of St. Stefan's Cathedral (bottom row, centre).

survivals in Vienna are the Lippizaner horses of the Spanish Riding School, which are put through dressage by riders dressed in brown, swallow-tail Spanish court uniforms, their wide-brimmed hats akin to those still worn by the Spanish police, the Guardia Civil.

Ferdinand I, following the now well-established Habsburg formula, managed to expand the eastern half of the empire by marriage and a large dose of good fortune. In 1521 he married Princess Anne, sister of Louis II, the last independent King of Bohemia and Hungary. At the time, Hungary was under the shadow of the Ottoman Turks, the most recent of the Asian powers to invade Europe. Louis died in battle against the Turks on the field of Mohács in August, 1526, and within a few months Ferdinand had secured his late brother-in-law's title to Bohemia and Hungary. Most of Hungary, however, was occupied by the Turkish infidels and the Austrians were now in the front line as defenders of Christendom.

For 150 years the outcome was in the balance, and twice Vienna was besieged. The first time was in 1529 when the Turks advanced from Hungary with an army of 250,000 and encamped in tens of thousands of tents around the city. For three weeks there was fierce fighting between besiegers and besieged. But the Viennese garrison held out, and when the winter snows began, the infidel horde retired into Hungary.

Ferdinand was able to arrange an uneasy truce with the Sultan, Suleiman the Magnificent. Until the end of the 17th Century, most of Hungary remained a Turkish province ruled by pashas. Turkish garrisons frequently skirmished against the Habsburgs, and treaties between Vienna and the Sultanate were more often broken than observed. Moreover, many of the Hungarian nobility, an anarchic lot at all times, preferred to ally themselves with Muslim Turks rather than the Catholic Habsburgs.

Eventually, this kind of Christian disarray encouraged the Ottoman Sultan to muster a huge army under his Vizier, Kara Mustafa, and to march once again on Vienna. In 1683 *Türkenglocken*, or bells sounding the alarm against the Turks, were rung in the city. The Emperor Leopold I left Vienna with his family and retreated up the Danube into Germany. He managed to obtain military help from many of the German princes—who rallied to the defence of the Habsburgs under the command of Charles, Duke of Lorraine—and from John Sobieski, King of Poland. Three months after the second siege of Vienna had begun, the combined Christian contingents arrived at Vienna, drove off the Turks and chased their vast and unwieldy army into Hungary. On Christmas Day, 1683, the unfortunate Kara Mustafa was strangled by order of the Sultan.

The victory was followed up by sustained military campaigns until the Turks were forced back into the Balkans. Finally, in 1699, by the Treaty of Karlowitz, the Ottoman Turks formally acknowledged the Habsburg title to Hungary. After the departure of the Turks, no invaders from the east made a comparable onslaught on Vienna until 1945 when the

A Chronicle of Power and Decline

c. A.D. 100	**Romans take over Celtic settlement at Vindobona; later fortify it and raise it to status of municipium, a city with the privileges of Roman citizenship**
c. 455	**Barbarian invaders settle in area now known as Austria**
795	**Charlemagne conquers the Avars and brings Austria within the bounds of his empire**
1156	**Austria becomes duchy, with Vienna as residence of its ruler, Heinrich Jasomirgott of Babenberg. Construction of St. Stefan's Cathedral begins**
1221	**Municipal and trading privileges granted to Vienna by Duke Leopold VI of Babenberg**
1246	**Death of Frederick the Warrior brings Babenberg dynasty to an end. He is succeeded by Ottokar II, King of Bohemia, who starts construction of Vienna's Hofburg Palace**
1278	**Emperor Rudolf of Habsburg defeats King Ottokar on the Marchfeld, gains Vienna and makes it his capital**
1365	**University of Vienna founded by Duke Rudolf IV**
1433	**Tower of St. Stefan's completed**
1469	**Vienna becomes seat of a bishop**
1477	**Archduke Maximilian of Habsburg marries Mary, heiress to Burgundy**
1493	**Maximilian elected Holy Roman Emperor as Maximilian I**
1496	**Philip, son of Emperor Maximilian I, marries Joanna of Castille, heiress to Spain**
1498	**Emperor Maximilian I founds court choristers, forerunners of Vienna Boys Choir**
1526	**Louis II Jagellon, King of Bohemia and Hungary, dies fighting the Turks at battle of Mohács. His brother-in-law, Archduke Ferdinand of Austria, is elected King of Bohemia and Hungary, marking the start of Habsburg domination in Central Europe**
1529	**First unsuccessful siege of Vienna by the Turks under Suleiman the Magnificent**
1572	**Emperor Maximilian II founds Spanish Riding School**
1620	**Battle of White Mountain, outside Prague, confirms authority of Habsburgs in Central Europe. Protestants expelled from Bohemia and Moravia**
1683	**Second siege of Vienna by Turks under Grand Vizier, Kara Mustafa, ends in rout of the Turks by combined German and Polish armies. Habsburg reconquest of Hungary begins under Charles of Lorraine and Eugene of Savoy**
1683-1740	**Great era of baroque palace and church building**
1718	**First Viennese porcelain factory founded**
1723	**Palaces of Lower and Upper Belvedere completed for Prince Eugene of Savoy**
1740	**Maria Theresa ascends Habsburg throne at age of 23. Wars against Frederick the Great of Prussia begin, embroiling Europe for more than 20 years**
1749	**Schönbrunn Palace completed by Nicholas Pacassi**
1766	**Prater, former imperial game reserve, becomes a public park**
1780-90	**Reforming Emperor Joseph II rules in Vienna, granting patent of religious tolerance and freedom of the Press**
1791	**Mozart dies in Vienna, unmourned**
1805	**Vienna occupied by the French after Battle of Austerlitz is won by Napoleon's forces**
1806	**Dissolution of Holy Roman Empire. Its last Emperor, Francis II, restyles himself Francis I of Austria**

1809 Habsburg forces defeat French at Aspern and are then defeated by French at Wagram. Composer Joseph Haydn dies in Vienna during second French occupation of city

814-15 At Congress of Vienna, statesmen of Austria, Russia, Prussia and Great Britain redraw map of Europe after Napoleonic Wars

815-48 Prince Metternich, successively Foreign Minister and Chancellor of Austria, suppresses liberal activists. Biedermeier art flourishes

1827 Beethoven dies and is buried in Währing cemetery at edge of city

1848 During spring revolution, Metternich and Habsburgs flee from Vienna. In autumn, Habsburg forces bombard city and regain power. Franz Josef becomes Emperor

1857 Franz Josef decrees demolition of medieval walls and fortifications to make way for Ringstrasse development

1867 Austrian Empire restyled as Austro-Hungarian Empire. Johann Strauss composes The Blue Danube

1869 Opera House, first public building on the Ring, inaugurated with performance of Mozart's Don Juan

871-75 River Danube is canalized

1881 Construction of new wing of the Hofburg Palace begins

1889 Archduke Rudolf, heir to the throne, commits suicide at Mayerling

1897 Giant Ferris wheel erected in Prater park. Gustav Mahler becomes Director of Vienna Opera, remaining in post for 10 years

1902 Sigmund Freud becomes professor at University of Vienna

906-13 Adolf Hitler lives in Vienna as poor student and labourer

1908 Annexation of Bosnia-Herzegovina, last Habsburg acquisition, generates renewed tension in Balkans

1914 Archduke Franz Ferdinand, heir to Habsburg throne, assassinated at Sarajevo by Bosnian student. Emperor Franz Josef signs declaration of war against Serbia, precipitating First World War

1916 Franz Josef dies and is succeeded by his great-nephew, Archduke Charles

1918 End of First World War and collapse of Habsburg Monarchy. At Schönbrunn, Charles renounces the throne, bringing to an end more than 600 years of Habsburg rule. Socialist Karl Renner becomes first Chancellor of Austrian Republic

920-34 64,000 workers' flats built by municipality of Vienna

1934 At climax of clashes between Left and Right, Chancellor Engelbert Dollfuss suppresses socialists, but is assassinated by Austrian Nazis

1938 Hitler annexes Austria. Many socialists and Jews flee Vienna

1945 Vienna bombed and Austria occupied by Allies at end of Second World War. Establishment of Second Republic

1955 State Treaty, signed in Upper Belvedere Palace, restores Austrian independence. Rebuilt Opera House opens with performance of Beethoven's Fidelio

1969 Socialist Bruno Kreisky becomes Chancellor. Strategic Arms Limitation Talks (SALT) open in Vienna. Construction of Vienna's underground railway begins

1973 Building of United Nations City, an office complex for 4,500 members of U.N. staff, gets under way

Soviets, with Mongolian and Kalmuck troops, followed Kara Mustafa's path, and went one better than him by occupying the city.

Military victories over foreign invaders were good for Habsburg prestige, but they were not sufficient to secure the Habsburg Empire. The subject peoples had to be governed, and that was no easy task. The Hungarians remained fiercely independent in spirit: they had a language, culture and history of which they were proud, and they rose regularly against the Habsburgs, most bloodily in 1848 under their patriotic leader Lajos Kossuth. Eventually, in 1867, a compromise was reached whereby Hungary was considered an equal and independent partner with Austria in the Austro-Hungarian Empire or Dual Monarchy. Under the terms of the agreement, the Emperor of Austria remained the King of Hungary, but the Hungarians enjoyed self-government through a parliament of their own in Budapest. When the empire collapsed in 1918, the Hungarians took their national independence as by right.

The Czechs, like the Hungarians, were proud of their heritage. In Prague, they had built one of the finest Gothic cathedrals in Europe, as well as the first university in Central Europe. To complicate matters, the Czechs converted to Protestantism during the Reformation, while the Habsburgs remained the most Catholic of rulers. In the end, Czech Protestantism—and with it Czech identity—had to be subdued by force of arms, an objective bloodily achieved in 1620 at the Battle of the White Mountain, so called after a hill on the outskirts of Prague. It was one of the decisive moments of the Thirty Years War, that conflict between Catholic Europe and Protestant Europe which lasted from 1618 to 1648. But Czech nationalism, although cowed, was never eradicated. It was to gain renewed strength in the 19th Century, and in 1918 its objectives were achieved when Czechoslovakia became independent under Thomas Masaryk, its first President.

In addition to Czechs and Hungarians, numerous other peoples of determined character were embraced as the empire grew, until eventually the list became dangerously long. To the south, there were the Croats, Slovenes, and Serbs—all inhabitants of present-day Yugoslavia, all perpetually at loggerheads with each other, and with the neighbouring Germans and Hungarians, and the Italians in the Habsburg provinces of Lombardy and Venetia. Italians were perhaps the most unsettling element in the empire, and many historians think that the Habsburg resources spent on policing them seriously weakened the empire. There were, besides, Poles and Ruthenes in the province of Galicia in the north-east, and Romanians in the eastern province of Transylvania. Coping with these minorities proved to be the essential Habsburg art of government.

There was, however, a glorious imperial interlude before nationalism really began to bite. In 18th-Century Vienna, when Turks no longer posed any external threat, the arts of peace could begin to rival the arts

On a grey afternoon, swallows sweep past Schönbrunn, a 1,200-room palace built for one of the greatest Habsburgs, the 18th-Century Empress Maria Theresa.

Elegantly dressed in velvet and lace, Empress Elizabeth of Austria-Hungary sits with her favourite dog, Shadow, in 1867. Her 45-year marriage to Franz Josef, which began with almost fairytale bliss, was eventually marked by tensions caused by her dislike of the rigidity of court life, a domineering mother-in-law, and her husband's compulsive preoccupation with work. In 1898 the Empress was murdered by an Italian anarchist in Geneva.

of war. Vienna became a city both grand and cosmopolitan. Anyone with an interest in power and patronage wished to be at the Habsburg court. Magnates like the Schwarzenbergs, the Lobkowitzes, Liechtensteins and Esterházys left the lands from which they derived their income and handed them over to be managed by others while they themselves, as ministers or ambassadors, managed affairs on behalf of their emperor. Each of the magnates felt impelled to build a *Stadtpalais*, a town palace, as close to the Hofburg and as much like it as possible, although in most cases scaled down appropriately.

It was Vienna's good fortune to enter its era of confidence at a time when Baroque architecture was at its best. There were two architects of genius at work in the city during the 18th Century: Johann Fischer von Erlach and Lukas von Hildebrandt. Both men were Italian-inspired. In their view, a noble style depended upon the study of classical antecedents, upon heroic portals, urns, statuary, and fountains writhing with tritons and dolphins. "Baroque" says it, in a word.

It was symbolic of the times that Prince Eugene of Savoy, who had risen to pre-eminence in the struggle against the Turks, should boldly have raised his palace, the Belvedere, in meadows outside the city, which at the start of the century was still confined within its medieval walls. The Belvedere, designed by Lukas von Hildebrandt, included ceremonial halls and reception rooms of marble and gilt, with a variety of plasterwork and carving (and statues of chained Turks thrown in for good measure). It represents the epitome of aristocratic taste—luxurious and carefree, truly fit for a prince. Almost too fit, indeed, for when Prince

Eugene died in 1736 without heirs, the Habsburgs judged it prudent never to let any subject of theirs live in the Belvedere again.

Visitors to 18th-Century Vienna noted how agreeable and amusing the city was. Lady Mary Montagu, a witty woman whose husband was British Ambassador to Turkey, stopped for a while in Vienna in 1716, and commented on the pleasant cosmopolitanism of the city. The Austrians, in her view, were not the most polite people in the world, nor the most agreeable. "But Vienna is inhabited by all nations, and I had formed myself a little society of such as were perfectly to my own taste." Remarking on the number of grand houses which had lately been built, she observed that retainers and tradesmen and all kinds of humble people were allowed a room or two on the landing alongside the noble owner, and that one and all rubbed shoulders amiably—an early example of the legendary Viennese cosiness, *Gemütlichkeit.*

The dominant figure of 18th-Century Vienna was Maria Theresa, an autocrat, but one with the common touch. She ruled from 1740 to 1780 and gave the age its lasting character. She had no fewer than 16 children, one of them Marie Antoinette, who was to die on the scaffold in Paris as the wife of Louis XVI.

The monarch as housewife—that was Maria Theresa. In her management of the empire she was a model of domestic economy. She established a standing army, raised new taxes to pay for it, provided a bureaucracy to collect the taxes, founded academies and schools to train officers and administrators. She centralized, she rationalized, she even brought in new codes of law to define the rights of peasants and nobility alike. Her reign was one of the best examples of the Enlightenment, and had the requisite French stress.

Maria Theresa's homely personality and her respect for things French are reflected in Schönbrunn, the summer palace she modelled on the lines of Versailles. Fischer von Erlach designed the palace in its first form, but Maria Theresa had it enlarged and extensively modified between 1744 and 1749 by the architect Nicholas Pacassi (Nicholas von Pacassi, as the Viennese upgraded him). Unlike his predecessor, he was no master of the grandiose. For all its 1,200 rooms, his palace of Schönbrunn is nice and unassuming, almost *gemütlich*, with its yellow wash and its tiled roof. The intricate French gardens, topped by the Gloriette, a colonnade with classical arches, ought to be expressions of the absolute power of the ruling house, but somehow they are not, French stiffness having failed to take root in this soil.

Vienna in the 18th Century may have been safe from military dangers, but the frontiers of the empire were under pressure on all sides. Although the Habsburgs were keen to imitate French styles and tastes, their political relations with France swung from warm to very cold. French ambitions to expand into the Low Countries, Italy, and the German principalities clashed with Habsburg interests in western Europe. In eastern Europe, Prussian ambitions were even more disturbing. At the opening of Maria Theresa's reign in 1740, Frederick the Great of Prussia, then a fledgling monarch, had seized the province of Silesia from the Habsburgs. In the Seven Years' War from 1756 to 1763, Austria failed to regain Silesia, in spite of making alliances with both Russia and France against Prussia.

With hindsight, it is possible to see that Frederick the Great's victory over Austria marked a turning point for the Habsburgs. A new power had arisen to challenge the supremacy of Vienna in Central Europe, and more deadly than that, the new power was also German. A risk had been created that one day the Germanic people of Austria might transfer their loyalties to the rising star of Prussia. The Habsburgs had lost the initiative in Europe; they were on the defensive. Frederick was so detested in Vienna for having diminished Maria Theresa's inheritance that, long afterwards, he remained in Viennese eyes "falsely called the Great". This little joke was a symptom of a desire that grew stronger over the next 150 years—a desire not to look at facts. It was the sort of wishful thinking parodied in the 20th Century by the Hungarian playwright, Ferenc Molnar, who in one of his plays made an elderly aristocratic lady say she had just read a book establishing that Napoleon had never even existed.

For many years, Napoleon and all he stood for seemed a far more present danger to the Habsburgs than any threat of Prussian expansionism. The French Revolution of 1789 and the ensuing Revolutionary and Napoleonic Wars challenged the entire order of Europe. The French experience of social upheaval shocked Maria Theresa's son and heir, Joseph II, who reigned from 1780 to 1790. He had believed, like his mother, that human happiness was a matter of decree and could be legislated. The revolutionary violence revealed to him that other orders in society, and other peoples under his rule, would be satisfied only with a share of power, never mind at whose expense.

The brunt of the Napoleonic Wars was taken by the Emperor Francis I, a born survivor who ruled until 1835. As Napoleon's armies stormed Europe, the Marchfeld once again witnessed epic clashes, at Aspern and Wagram. In 1809, Napoleon occupied Vienna. Francis' was the classic dilemma of the weak: he could not defeat the French; he therefore had to submit with good grace, in the hope of mercy. For the good of the empire, he consented to the marriage of his daughter Marie Louise to Napoleon. The ceremony took place in the Augustinerkirche adjoining the Hofburg, but Napoleon was not even present. It was a marriage by proxy and Marie Louise's uncle, the Archduke Charles, stood in for the groom. The bride first met her husband in a carriage halfway to Paris.

Napoleon was, of course, ultimately defeated by the Quadruple Alliance of Austria, Britain, Prussia and Russia. The victors met at the Congress of Vienna and, in 1815, formalized the new peace of Europe, which was to

An aging Franz Josef (centre) attends the wedding reception in October, 1911, of his great-nephew Archduke Charles, seen standing by the bride, Princess Zita of Bourbon-Parma. Five years later, in the middle of the First World War, the Archduke became Emperor, but his reign was brief. In 1919 he went into exile, ending more than 600 years of Habsburg rule.

survive 99 years, until the hot summer of 1914. The Congress was a remarkable occasion, unprecedented in diplomacy and thought by its participants to have been unmatched anywhere for brilliance, festivity, wisdom and achievement. Meanwhile, Marie Louise had given birth to Napoleon's only son, who was known as the Duke of Reichstadt. He was brought up in the Hofburg, where his cradle is on show, and died young.

The Austrian Foreign Minister, Prince Metternich, had taken the credit for arranging the marriage of Napoleon and Marie Louise, and then for the Congress of Vienna. Having salvaged the empire, he was determined to avoid anything that might risk a revolution. A pessimist about human nature, Metternich did not believe in happy endings. Sophisticated and civilized, he wore the proverbial velvet glove that concealed the iron hand. He instituted censorship and set up a powerful secret police. Arbitrary and unconstitutional methods of this kind were able in the short run to suppress rebellion, but they gave the peoples of the empire a heightened awareness of their grievances.

Metternich's mistake was to treat as revolutionaries people who had come to see themselves as nationalists. A generation of Europeans had grown up enthusing over Byron's pleas for the liberation of Greece from the Turks, applauding the heroes of the wars of independence in South America, reading Pushkin's and Walter Scott's romancings of national character—in short, embracing the notion of manifest destiny for every people and every culture. The Habsburg Empire had become a collection of embryo nations, each with its own prophets. The Italians of Venetia and Lombardy had their patriotic leader, Giuseppe Mazzini. Hungarians

In the great hall of Schönbrunn, scarlet-and-gold military uniforms blend with gilt-and-velvet decor as the Emperor Franz Josef (centre, in grey) dines with officers of the Lifeguards. The Habsburg taste for pomp and circumstance survived to the very end of the imperial era; this banquet, painted by the Austrian artist Ludwig Koch, took place in December, 1913.

turned to Kossuth and the aristocratic statesman Count Széchenyi. The Czechs read their great nationalist historian Frantisek Palacký. Those of German origins within the empire were increasingly tempted to admire the thrust of the new Prussia.

Finally, in 1848, nationalistic uprisings broke out in Italy, in Budapest and in Prague. Viennese students demonstrated in favour of such elementary constitutional rights as freedom of speech, the establishment of a liberal parliament and the granting of a constitution. The government panicked. Prince Metternich fled to England.

Ferdinand, Emperor of Austria at the time, was known as Ferdinand the Kind, for kind he was—to the point of simplemindedness. He had been content to leave everything to Metternich. Like Metternich, he felt obliged to leave Vienna, and he sought refuge in Olmütz, in the province of Moravia. But one member of the family did not lose her head, and that was the Archduchess Sophie of Bavaria. Her son, the 18-year-old Franz Josef, was next in line to the throne after Ferdinand. She saw her chance, and took it. She got the army on her side and suppressed the revolution in Vienna. For the sake of solidarity between monarchs, the Russian Tsar was eager to lend troops to do what had to be done in Hungary.

Shootings and repression followed—and they were not to be forgotten within the empire. The conservatives were dismayed that they had been obliged to resort to these methods; in the future, they would be even more wary and resentful of any change. The liberals and revolutionaries wanted revenge. Ferdinand abdicated. On stepping down, he is supposed to have blessed his successor Franz Josef, stroked his cheek, and said, "Courage, my boy! You're welcome!" The heritage he had passed on looked unmanageable, and he was thankful to be rid of it.

Vienna, when we think of it, is even nowadays inescapably bound up with the figure of Franz Josef, just as the British Empire is with Queen Victoria. He reigned for 68 years, she for 63. The youthful Franz Josef looked the right man in the right place. Queen Victoria wrote down a vivid portrait of him during an official visit he made to London: "I like the Young Emperor, I must admit; there is much spirit and boldness in his warm blue eyes, and he shows a certain agreeable gaiety, when the occasion arises. He is slender and graceful, and even in the midst of dancers and archdukes, all in uniform, he can always be recognized as their head. There is a certain something about him that lends authority."

That certain something lasted throughout his life. He would be opposed, but he was never insulted. How and why things went wrong during his long rule—whether Franz Josef made false moves in the game of power politics, or whether the Habsburg decline was an ineluctable Greek tragedy—are questions that will always be debated. Outwardly, at least, Vienna showed signs of energy. The Industrial Revolution had begun in

Austria after the Congress of Vienna, and the economic impetus of steam power and factory production continued into Franz Josef's reign. New buildings for new institutions gave the city a work-site appearance. The construction of technical colleges, academies, laboratories, concert halls did justice to Vienna's reputation as one of the great capitals of Europe. Any Metternich-style belief in unhappy endings seemed to be dispelled. Hundreds of memoirs by people in all walks of life testify that the Vienna of Franz Josef had faith in itself: somehow the Emperor would see everyone through.

The facts hardly justified this feeling. The problem of nationalism became increasingly trying. To be forced to grant the wishes of one nationality was to be forced to grant the wishes of all. The Italians of Lombardy and Venetia demanded a more liberal constitution and national unity, and they backed up their demands by force of arms. The movement for the unification of Italy, led by the two men who had succeeded Mazzini as nationalist leaders, Giuseppe Garibaldi and Count Cavour, eventually succeeded in forcing the Austrians out of their Italian provinces, and the Kingdom of Italy was declared in 1861. Also, Prussia once more became a danger. In 1862 Otto von Bismarck was appointed Prime Minister of Prussia, and he, more than any other man, killed off the Habsburg Empire. His aim was to unify the German states under Prussia's leadership, and this re-arrangement of Central Europe could be done only at the expense of Austria; it was a matter, as Bismarck said with his customary magnetism, of "blood and iron".

He built up the finest fighting force on the continent. To provoke war, he then picked a footling quarrel about Austria's control of the Duchy of Holstein, and Franz Josef fell into the trap. At the battle of Königgrätz in July, 1866, the Austrian troops in their white uniforms marched into action in close formation behind their regimental bands, to be met by a new invention, the needle-gun, or breech-loading, quick-firing rifle. The white Austrian uniforms were spattered red immediately. Within seven weeks the Austro-Prussian war was over and Vienna was subordinated to Berlin as the capital of the German-speaking world.

The last decades before the First World War were a slow death-bed scene for the Habsburg Empire. Franz Josef maintained due grandeur, styling himself "Emperor of Austria, King of Hungary, of Bohemia, Dalmatia, Croatia, Slavonia, Galicia, Lodomeria and Illyria; King of Jerusalem, Archduke of Austria; Grand-duke of Tuscany and Cracow; Duke of Lorraine, of Salzburg, Styria, Carinthia, Carniola and Bukovina, Grand-duke of Transylvania . . ." as well as Duke, Count, Lord, and Margrave of innumerable other corners of Europe. The glory was about equal to the fiction.

The Emperor refused to be downcast. He kept up appearances. He bothered about the minutiae of administration; he memorized the names

The funeral of Emperor Franz Josef on November 30, 1916, was one of the last great state occasions of the Habsburg era. Despite the need for troops in the war effort, six of the Austro-Hungarian Army's seven companies of imperial guardsmen (shown in the photographs below) escorted the hearse to the Capuchin Church in the Neuer Markt, where the Emperor was laid to rest in the imperial vault, beside 137 of his Habsburg ancestors.

The Emperor's Gentlemen-at-Arms

Hungarian Lifeguards

Lifeguard Infantrymen

Austrian Special Lifeguards

Dismounted Lifeguard Cavalrymen

Hungarian Special Lifeguards

Six decades after the collapse of the Habsburg Empire, tribute to the Emperor Franz Josef has become an antiquarian trend. The stern eye and mutton-chops of the Grand Old Man reign on, whether carved in crystal (top left), exhibited on a pavement (top right), adorning a beaker (bottom left), or even emblazoned on the side of a van (bottom right).

of insignificant officials in Galicia or station-masters in Slovenia, and fretted about their promotions and loyalties. He toured the provinces, he inspected ceaselessly. His personal routine was more than spartan; it had about it an element of self-denial, as if he were taking upon himself the sins of his subjects, to save their souls. Up at six, and straight to the paperwork. Each day brought scores of audiences and appointments which were duly recorded in a huge black ledger. A light luncheon with a little white wine was served in his study. Then came parades, more inspections, an evening reception that bored him, or a court ball that bored him more, and early to bed. His demeanour was that of a father who loved all his fractious children equally.

The business, and the frugality, still astonish. His desk in the Hofburg, his few personal photographs, his whole study, his daily surroundings could not have been more modest. He slept on an iron-frame military bed (did he wish his subjects to perceive that his mission to rule contained personal punishment?). He continued to enjoy health and longevity. Silver wedding, golden jubilee, diamond jubilee passed. His good looks grew majestic as the big brow became bald and the compensating whiskers thickened and whitened. His subjects tended to imitate him, which was the sincerest flattery. They too grew whiskers and affected the imperial gravity. They too rose early and worked hard to accomplish little. A whole style evolved as the ruled took the imprint of their ruler.

Kaiserlich-Königlich was his traditional title: Imperial-Royal, commonly abbreviated to *k.k.* The "Imperial" referred to his position as Emperor of Austria, the "Royal" to his title over lands such as Bohemia. State institutions and officials and purveyors of goods to the Imperial-Royal family were dubbed *k.k.* However, after the establishment of the Dual Monarchy in 1867, *k.k.* was applied only to the Austrian half; institutions and officials serving both Austria and Hungary were termed *Kaiserlich und Königlich*, Imperial *and* Royal. The distinction was slight, but it represented a real concession to the Hungarians; and the abbreviated *k. und k.* became the proud hallmark of army and diplomacy.

The Old Gentleman, as Franz Josef was familiarly called, was a palpable presence at every Viennese occasion, public and private; respect flowed upwards to him. It hardly mattered whether or not he were there in person, dressed in his blue uniform—known with wonderful frenchified amusement as the "Bonjourl", or "Good-Day Outfit"—and wearing his cocked green hat with its dyed green plumes. At parades, he sat erect on his horse. Always correct, the Old Gentleman was a statue with locomotor powers, and the Viennese deferred to him as a wonder. People were not stupid, of course. They realized what was coming: the Old Gentleman's death would surely bring to a head all the calamities his life had suspended. There was nothing to be done except wait for the end as gaily and courageously as possible.

The Old Gentleman was also respected for what he had suffered. His marriage had not been happy. His wife Elizabeth was a princess of the ancient Wittelsbach family of Bavaria, and a streak of madness ran in the line. Had there not been ill omens at their wedding when his sword had fallen and her veil had slipped? He called her Sissi. He adored her and wanted to spare her shocks, while making a figurehead of her. Because of her beauty, her youthfulness, her white skin and dark hair in braids, it is easy to romanticize her as the ideal empress. But she seems to have been out of her depth in affairs of state. She found her in-laws intolerable; she shirked public duties to the point of rudeness, snubbing her husband when he pleaded with her to make official appearances. She preferred to ride, and did so obsessively, hunting with one pack of fox-hounds after another, as if to gallop away from it all. She might have loved Franz Josef if he had not been so kind to her, so virtuous. She certainly cared for him in her fashion; she even arranged for him to have a confidante, Frau Katharina Schratt, an actress in the Burgtheater, who poured tea for the Emperor in her flat and listened to him with propriety.

In the chill suites of the Hofburg is a room where the Empress did her gymnastic exercises. On the walls are her pictures of the animals she loved: her white horses Flick and Flock; her dogs, mostly mastiffs and boxers with names like Dragon, Bravo, Oscar, Hamlet. Franz Josef built a pavilion for her in a park at Lainz, on the edge of the city, where she was supposed to be able to ride by herself to her heart's content. Woundingly, she hardly ever went there. She did the minimum compatible with her position. When finally, in 1898, she was assassinated by a madman on the shore of Lake Geneva, to which she had retired as though separated, the Emperor's loneliness was sealed.

In one important respect—perhaps the most important, where the future of Vienna was concerned—her hopes had already come to nothing. Her one son, Rudolf, the Crown Prince, heir to the throne, had killed himself at the age of 31 on a January night in 1889. With his 18-year-old mistress, Marie Vetsera, he had gone to his hunting-lodge at Mayerling, in the Helenental valley outside Vienna. And there shots were heard in the small hours. When the bedroom door was broken down, both lovers were found dead, in a suicide pact. The motives have never been cleared up. Perhaps Rudolf had inherited a streak of Wittelsbach madness; perhaps he had syphilis; perhaps Marie Vetsera was his illegitimate sister, and someone had finally told him—explanations have been many and ingenious, but without enough benefit of facts.

Who could fail to be sorry for the Old Gentleman? His own brother, Maximilian, had been invited in 1864 by Mexican traditionalists to become King of Mexico, which was then just emerging from civil war; but after a brief rule he was put before a firing-squad by Mexican revolutionaries. The Old Gentleman despised the nephew—Archduke Franz Ferdinand, a self-important figure—who had become his heir after Rudolf's death. It was a bitter irony that, in 1914, the Emperor had to mobilize his armies to avenge the murder of this nephew by Serbian nationalists in Sarajevo. When Austria declared war on Serbia, whose government was thought to be responsible for the assassination, Russia sprang to Serbia's defence, France sprang to Russia's side, Germany declared war on Russia and France, Britain declared war on Germany, and the First World War began. As the Old Gentleman lamented, "Nothing has been spared me". But in that he was wrong. Dying in 1916, he was still in time to be buried in state, as he should have been, instead of being hustled away in extreme old age and ignominy to a grave in exile.

In one place in Vienna, a few salvaged shreds and tatters of Habsburg glory can still be seen—in the old Arsenal in the southern outskirts of the city. Here, in dozens of warehouses covering an enormous area, were stored the arms and munitions which had to be provided for the Imperial and Royal army, usually on several fronts at once, thereby draining the strength of the empire. Of all careers, the military was the proudest and most respected, so much so that the bureaucracy and the professions emulated it, creating cast-iron distinctions of rank and demanding strict obedience from juniors.

The central block of the Arsenal complex has been converted into a military museum; and more than that, into an epitaph. It has a weird and wonderful appearance: red-brick, castellated and crenellated, with arabesque appurtenances. Huge pillars in the entrance hall are adorned with the statues of the empire's heroes, figures so outsize that their calves are at eye-level, and their heads far above, loftily beyond mere mortal scope. A great ceremonial staircase rises, its varied marbling and frescos resplendent. The vaulted ceiling shines with gilding, and below hang scores of the outdated and outlawed yellow Habsburg banners with the black double-headed eagle. Around the walls of the first-floor lobbies are tablets to commemorate the illustrious dead, whose epitaphs recall the variety of the empire and its military encounters: Graf zu Eckh und Hungersbach, died at Cardona, 1711; Bartholomäus von Andia-Irrau Irradazzaval, Marquis von Valparayso, Graf von Villaverde, died at Guastalla, 1734; Franz Wenzel Graf Desfours zu Mont und Athienville, died at Czaslaw, 1742; Anton Freiherr Formestini von Tulmein und Bignin, died at Liegnitz, 1760. There are hundreds more of these forgotten soldiers of fortune, mostly minor aristocrats from Spain, Italy, even France, who enlisted under those banners and fell in forgotten battles. The Habsburg cause was prepared to accept anyone; the one thing these men have in common is that they were persuaded to die for it.

In showcases are the head-dresses of Hussars, Dragoons, Cuirassiers, Uhlans, Deutsche Kavallerie and the famous Hoch-und-Deutschmeister

Regiment. Nothing is left of the Habsburg armies but these bits of dashing finery. On a wall hangs a picture—not a very good picture, but poignant for all that—of a banquet scene in the Great Hall of Schönbrunn, showing Franz Josef dining with his gentlemen-at-arms, the *Arcièren-Leibgarde*, to celebrate the 150th anniversary of the regiment. In a sea of scarlet uniforms, the painter has managed to pick out each figure at the long table, seizing his formality and the detail of his military attitude, down to the monocle. And the date? December 29, 1913. It could equally well have been 1813, so little had the *k. und k.* world changed.

In a room of its own is the motor car in which the Archduke Franz Ferdinand and his wife were being driven when they were shot at Sarajevo. The coach-work bears a hole made by one of the bullets that brought down court, army, *Arcièren-Leibgarde*, throne and even Europe as it had been. This car did not even belong to the thrifty Habsburgs, but to a Count Harrach who had lent it for the occasion, and never got it back.

And there is one last living testimony to the aims and achievements of the empire, in—of all places—the Vienna telephone book. At first it seems just a pastime to pick out the names, as from a hat, for their exotic sound: Strusievici, Chromecki, Morari, Tschuggel, Has, Hrdlitschka, Artinjak, Prkic, Hunyady, Szczepankiewicz, Wolosobe. Here is a more systematic selection from a single page: "Crikl, Cvrk, Cweyn, Cwick, Cybulewski, Cycha, Cyganivk, Cyhlar, Cymbalnik, Czada, Czallarn, Czaritz, Czasch, Czechaczek, Czechovsky." Or, again: "Nedomansky, Nedomlel, Nedwed, Nedzka, Neeb, Neff, Neffzern, Nefischer, Negilink, Negratschker, Negrelli, Negrey, Neheschleb, Nehez." But I must stop, because this is an unfinished symphony. These are the descendants of people who, in all their colour and variety, were brought under Habsburg sway. They grumbled at the time, all those finicky minorities, but in the end they found safe shelter in Vienna; and the telephone book testifies to the cosmopolitan ideal which the Habsburgs did their imperfect best to create.

The Precise Art of the Lippizaners

A horseman wearing the school's traditional uniform—cutaway coat, jodhpurs and bicorne hat—trains a stallion to perform the stiff-legged Spanish trot.

One of the few surviving reminders of the days when the Habsburgs ruled Spain as well as Austria is Vienna's Spanish Riding School. The purpose of this unique institution is, in the words of a former director, "to retain and cultivate the art of horsemanship in its highest form". The Spanish connection dates from the 16th Century, when Iberian bloodstock was brought to Lippiza, now in Yugoslavia, to start the dynasty of "Lippizaner" horses that the school still breeds in Austria today. Stallions selected for training spend most of the year stabled in the Stallburg, a section of the Hofburg Palace situated just a few paces from the splendid baroque hall known as the Winter Riding School. There, to musical accompaniment, the world-famous Lippizaners give Sunday morning performances of their choreographed equestrian art.

A stallion on its way to exercise passes a stall marked with a brass nameplate and overlooked by a stone bust.

Rows of saddles—some of white buckskin for performances, others of brown leather for training—line a wall in the Stallburg tack-room.

Stable-boys lead four Lippizaners through the Stallburg's Renaissance courtyard. A sculpture from the Kunsthistorisches Museum collection stands in shadow.

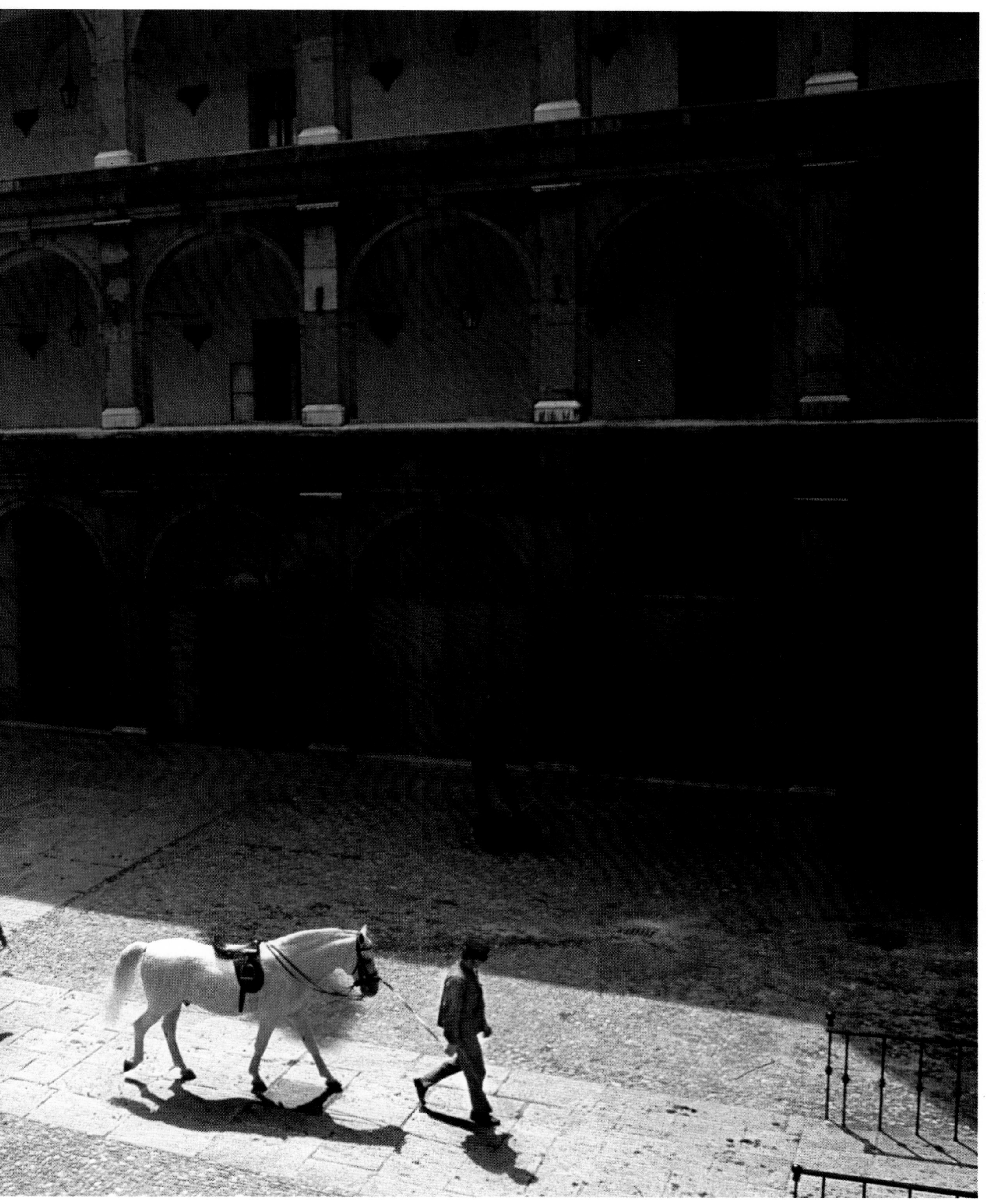

During a workout in the Winter Riding School, a trainer keeps a high-stepping Lippizaner on a long rein while preparing it for the stationary trot called the Piaffe.

Mastering the Classical Steps

To enable them to develop freely, the Lippizaners receive no training until they are three-and-a-half years old. Once the process begins, however, it is intensive. During their first two years of tutelage, they are broken in and learn to move with a supple gait. Only in the third year do they start work on the elaborate series of steps and movements known as *Haute Ecole*, of which the School's horses and riders are the world's best-known exponents.

A horse practising the complicated movement called "the half pass to the left" moves forward diagonally, crossing its forelegs as it goes.

The goat-like leap called the Capriole is the showpiece of a Lippizaner's solo performances. As shown in the sequence of photographs above, the horse starts the movement on its haunches, then, springing upwards, gathers its hind legs for a backward kick (right) performed in mid-air.

Beneath the chandeliers of the Winter Riding School, eight Lippizaners mesmerize a packed house with the balletic sequence known as the School Quadrille.

3

The Well-tempered Life

I am trapped in the maze of one-way streets that is the Fourth District. There seems to be a conspiracy to prevent me from driving into the Favoritenstrasse at the point where I want to be. I am forced up to the Südbahnhof, or into the Wiedner Hauptstrasse and down to the Ring. In between, I zig-zag at the mercy of stern arrows and no-entry signs. There is nowhere to park the car and so I abandon it recklessly, trusting my British licence plate to protect me from the Viennese traffic wardens. On the dashboard I already have a specimen of what must be the most courteous parking tickets in the world, a little *billet-doux* addressed to *"Sehr geehrter Fahrzeuglenker"*. I hardly feel like a "highly-esteemed vehicle-steersman", as I run for it. An appointment has been made for me at 10 o'clock with the director of the Theresianum, the old and very Catholic school that trained and still trains the élite of the country. I am going to be a good five minutes late. This is a punctual city, and so disgrace is looming. Ahead I can see, at last, the façade of the famous school, a noble yellow in colour, with a baroque swell to it. I sprint to the entrance. The porter in his lodge does his best not to look startled.

A lot of trouble went into the making of this appointment. The previous week I had dined with friends. All of them wanted to know what kind of book I would write about Vienna. So enclosed is the city that I had the feeling each light remark of mine at dinner set ten thousand telephones purring the next day: "So that's what he's after." Whatever I replied, however I stalled, I could practically hear them wincing. Had I been to the Town Hall, they wanted to know? If I said yes, then they assumed that I was falling into the hands of the socialists who are so skilful at public relations and propaganda. Or had the conservatives got hold of me, to promote their views about the commanding heights of private enterprise and the perseverance of traditional culture? If I said yes to that, then I must be an old-fashioned reactionary. What made them uneasy, above all, was that I should be independent and making up my own mind.

The Theresianum had been mentioned. One of those present happened to be president of its Old Boys Association. He is descended from a princely family, but must now make do with the plainer title of *Doktor*—properly earned in his case, though pronounced with a pinch of extra emphasis just to show that really it signifies Prince and that lip service to modern republicanism goes just so far, *but no farther*. He had been kind enough to put me in touch with the school's director, who scrambled through his diary for a spare hour—and now here I was trying to get my breath back

In the restaurant of the famous Hotel Sacher, a waiter pauses, ice bucket at the ready, beneath the gaze of Frau Anna Sacher, who owned the hotel a century ago. The Sachers are gone now —Anna, a tough cigar-smoking lady, died in 1930—but the establishment retains the plush formality that characterized imperial Vienna.

as I climbed a handsome stone staircase, trotted behind the porter down an echoing corridor and was ushered into an ante-chamber.

A crucifix adorned its walls, otherwise bare except for a travel poster or two. In a small cubby-hole of an inner office, partitioned off, a secretary was quietly reading a novel. He nodded. I sat on one of those brown chairs whose spindliness suggests disapproval of the weight about to be placed on them. A big door led into the director's office and on its far side boomed the director's voice. He was having a telephone conversation. Up a tone, down a tone. I asked the secretary whether it would not be well to slip the director a message that I had arrived. My suggestion was highly unwelcome. The secretary pointed to a lighted red button on his desk; when it flicked off, he explained, the telephoning would be over and he would announce me. To interrupt someone as important as the director, even wordlessly with a slip of paper, was unheard-of.

Fifteen minutes passed, and then thirty, forty-five. The secretary put down his novel and confronted me. "Waiting," he said by way of explanation, "is the prime duty of every citizen." Two schoolboys crept in, straight away summed up the situation and crept out. At the fifty-five minute mark—with the fatal button still red—my allotted time was nearly up; besides, I had another appointment. So, greatly daring, I ignored the secretary and pushed open the door to express regrets and announce my departure.

Not a bit of it. The director hung up the receiver, and without any reference to the time, placed himself entirely at my service. His helpfulness soon made it impossible for me to think of keeping my second appointment. But the director too had another appointment: to see the mother of a boy who had had an unfortunate clash with the chemistry master. She, meanwhile, had occupied my brown chair. She was dressed in black, as though putting on widow's weeds to mourn her son's possible expulsion and blighted prospects. Poor woman: she waited in that ante-chamber until she could stand it no more; and then, when the director took me on a tour of the school, she hovered like a wraith in the courtyard or in a schoolroom where we were sure to notice her. "Just a moment longer," the director would say to her, raising a plump and calming hand.

I felt I was being used as an instrument to torment her, just as the telephone had been used to torment me. Asia, in the famous remark of Prince Metternich, begins on the Landstrasse, one of the roads leading out of Vienna to the east; and here was one of those characteristic assertions of despotic power. In thousands of offices all over the city that very morning, similar scenes demonstrating one man's power over another were being enacted. Soul after soul is damned to endure the daily course of bureaucratic encounters in dusty, file-bound ministries; each is trapped in hierarchies that have scarcely altered in appearance, never mind character, since Metternich's day a century and a half ago. Quite to Metternich's taste would be the enduring absolutism that every Viennese

In her ladylike Sunday best, a little girl stands on tiptoe to see a religious street procession. Like most well brought-up Viennese children, she has learned at an early age to be correctly dressed for important occasions.

in office, from President to clerk, seems bound to assert over everyone of lesser status, or in temporary need of his services.

The Theresianum is Old Vienna. During the 17th Century, it had been an imperial castle and residence. The Emperor Charles VI, father of Maria Theresa, had lived and died there. His small bedroom on the first floor is now a chantry chapel. Maria Theresa spent her childhood there; but with new Schönbrunn to move into, she offered the place to the Jesuits as a school where civil servants could be trained for the empire, which was then being overhauled, rationalized and centralized. That is the origin of the Theresianum.

There are just over 500 boys in the school, of whom a fifth are boarders. In addition to the normal syllabus required for state examinations, the pupils must study Latin, English, French and Russian, plus the sciences. The compulsory emphasis on languages derives from the presence next door, along the Favoritenstrasse, of the Diplomatische Akademie. Candidates for the foreign service can be groomed in the Theresianum's complex of school buildings from the age of eight onwards; and if that does not produce "the right type", nothing will.

The boarders are divided into groups, each with a master as a kind of cheer-leader or moral tutor. They sleep in dormitories and eat in a splendidly ornate dining-room, like a college hall. As a reading-room they can use the Bibliotheca Theresiana, an unspoilt 18th-Century library; on the librarian's desk still stands a framed photograph of the Emperor Franz Josef. Anybody who has ever been inside an English public school will recognize this atmosphere, with its spirit of *mens sana in corpore sano.* It is a very strong mould. In the normal course of events it induces self-confidence, and it gives undoubted personal advantages to the lucky few.

The Theresianum represents the kind of compromise between the demands of the past, present and future at which the Austrians excel. The teaching staff is paid by the state, but administration is in the hands of the Curatorium, or Board of Regents, whose members tend to be former pupils. The traditionalists can thus argue that they have managed to maintain the values of private education without paying much of a price.

On my way round the school I dropped in on the Chairman of the Board of Regents, an elegant retired civil servant. He has 18th-Century rooms for his offices and, in keeping with orthodox Habsburg taste, the white plasterwork has been picked out with gilt and the fine furniture upholstered in red silk. He explained to me that the Theresianum had owned estates in Czechoslovakia until they were confiscated by the communist government in 1948. The school still has farmland and forests near Vienna, and in the provinces of Lower Austria and Styria, but the income from those sources is not sufficient. The state recognizes its obligation to make good the school's deficit, given the educational objectives. "The aim is to build up personality, not in order to have more

This portrait of a musical Viennese family, by an unknown artist of the 1840s, expresses the essence of domestic harmony—a song recital in the drawing-room. The painter has perfectly captured the snug prosperity of the early 19th-Century period known as Biedermeier, after a character in some contemporary comic poems.

rights but more duties. Service—that's the point. Our curriculum is special, but the state approves it."

It was well past lunch-time before my guided tour was over. That poor mother in black, importuning the director at every turn, was an eloquent sight. At last the director turned to her and she could begin handwringing on her son's behalf, with a rush of pleas to spare him the awful disgrace of expulsion merely because he and the chemistry master did not hit it off.

What the Theresianum brings into focus are the mysteries of egalitarianism as practised in modern Vienna. How can this aristocratic education be made to square with another school, buried out of sight in the poorer 20th district, into which I accidentally poked my head on a winter's day? Snow had come on, the temperature had been falling, and Vienna had suddenly developed into a mammoth skating-rink of ice. Only one garage, apparently, sold chains to fit the tyres of my car, and so I went to hunt it out in a very squalid patch of old buildings. The most leprous of these buildings had German Gothic inscriptions over the door, proclaiming that it was a high school. I entered. There was a nasty smell, overcrowding, kids squabbling, dinginess, deprivation. Perhaps this school was as untypical as the Theresianum, but between the two there could never be any question of equal opportunity. Yet the same ministry is responsible for both, and that ministry calls itself socialist.

No doubt about it, the crueller distinctions of class have long since been smoothed over. Virtually everybody will claim with pride and pleasure that class barriers have become a thing of the past and that Vienna is social democracy at its blossoming best. And true enough, Vienna is social democratic—even socialist—in externals, in forms, in appearance. People in the streets are well dressed and well fed, alike in all visible respects; the poor not all that poor, the rich not all that rich. In public nobody is going to be bold enough to stand on privilege or on talent.

And yet very little of this external equality translates into daily conduct such as being nice and informal with one another. The Viennese simply do not treat each other as social democratic equals. They want what they can get for themselves, and correspondingly expect others to keep for themselves whatever they can. Nobody seems to challenge the continued existence of the Theresianum, just as nobody seems to feel that the slum school is a disgrace. It is as if everyone carried the ancient pecking order of the Habsburg centuries so fixedly in his head that there is no need to institutionalize it or even mention it. One just knows one's place.

Upon meeting someone of superior station, a Viennese instinctively inclines his head and shoulders quite deeply, casts his eyes down to the floor, and surreptitiously straightens his legs to attention: a gesture of deference where deference is due. Franz Josef would still feel very much at home. The result of this inherited class awareness is that daily life becomes a complex process of bargaining about status that is often amusing, always curious, and sometimes a little pitiful.

To begin at the top, the aristocracy has compromised very little with the present. They still form a clan and still practise those manners that once were a byword in Europe. Those with estates in Czechoslovakia and Hungary were dispossessed by post-war communist governments there, but anyone with property in Austria itself has been able to make good money out of agriculture and forestry. The taxation system in Austria is not weighted against the landed interest; on the contrary, the state readily gives grants to enable owners of historic houses to restore them and live in them. Many a son finds he has been able to recapture a position which he thought his father had abandoned forever.

At a shoot I attended in the country, every one of the guests was a member of an aristocratic family. Their grandfathers had been to occasions just like this in 1900. No industrialist, no nouveau riche had cracked the magic circle. The sporting wives were so many mannequins for English hand-made boots, Italian scarves, sheepskin coats, shooting sticks, the complete *comme il faut* gear.

The gamekeepers and beaters addressed the guests and their wives by their former titles and deferred to them with the politeness of old-fashioned servants. The only sign of the times was lunch, when everyone—guests and gamekeepers alike—sat down at the same long table, ate

On the day of the annual Grand Prix at Freudenau, a racegoer watches the passing parade from a private box.

Racecourse Chic

Horse-racing in Vienna, as in other great capitals, has a significant place in the social calendar. After all, it is still called the sport of kings. To the Viennese, a day at the Freudenau—the fashionable racecourse in the enormous Prater park on the east side of the city—is an occasion for seeing and being seen. The course, founded in 1868, was a rendezvous of the aristocracy for the first 50 years of its existence, and men would usually attend in their military uniforms. Twentieth-century Viennese find the attractions of a day at the races as irresistible as ever, and although the racegoers nowadays come from every social background, their commitment to elegance remains undiminished.

Racecourse dandies sport fashionable moustaches and custom-made suits.

A dapper gentleman uses a monocle as well as glasses to study a programme.

In a private enclosure, a pair of society matrons make earnest conversation, while sober-suited owners wait for the horses to be led out for saddling.

A frowning spectator brings intense concentration—and high-powered binoculars—to bear on the problem of picking potential winners in the paddock.

Bemedalled army officers mingle with other representatives of the Viennese beau monde behind wrought-iron railings in one of the smart enclosures.

the same food and shared in the same general conversation. However, none of the gamekeepers would have considered omitting a guest's title, nor would the guest have offered to drop it either.

This kind of class equilibrium depends upon people doing what is expected of them. Anyone who does not conform is quickly given the impression that he is challenging the system, whether he intended to or not. I met a count who had been brought up in America after the last war. Then he came into his inheritance—a dilapidated estate and a castle that had fallen into ruin while occupied by Soviet troops. Taking stock of the situation after his return, he borrowed money to modernize the farming and the forestry, and rolled up his sleeves. When necessary, he drives the tractor and logs the trees himself. Capitalizing on his assets, he also lets the shooting rights profitably. Hideous faux-pas. Nobody in his family, in his entire background, had done anything commercial for as long as records have been kept. His grandfather sent for him and issued a warning that he was sullying the family's good name. To the old man, choosing between cash and tradition was no choice at all. By breaking the code—even though all he is doing is adapting to changing circumstances—the young count loses respect among his kind.

Better by far to be the old Viennese character I know, of whom it has been pleasantly said that he did nothing for 20 years except saunter up and down the Kärntnerstrasse, which runs between the Ring and St. Stefan's Cathedral and therefore could not be more central and smart. This description of his life is perfectly well understood by upper and lower-class Viennese to mean that he was taking honourable advantage of the pleasures of being rich.

Such are the easy-going manners that every Viennese still consciously aspires to. What is the grand life about if not procedure, etiquette? Practise the etiquette, then, and the grand life is there to command—for proletariat and bourgeoisie alike.

It is not a coincidence that the stock figure of Viennese opera and operetta, from Mozart to Johann Strauss, is a servant disguised as his master. Mozart's Leporello or Figaro realize that they cannot succeed in passing themselves off as Don Giovanni or Count Almaviva, but they have observed the higher conduct well enough to have a crack at it, well enough to hope that parody may merge into the real thing. This has been the dream of the many thousands of simple folk who, over the last two centuries, have forsaken the land and begun to climb the unfriendly urban ladder to prosperity and respectability. And the more the Viennese are squeezed together by modern pressures, the harder they strive to draw infinitesimal gradations of class. That's the paradox of this socialist society; and it is loveable or hateful according to your temperament.

Much fun is poked at the Viennese passion for high-flown titles that describe their jobs and their status. It's good for a laugh when two acquaintances stop on the street, raise their hats and address each other with circumspect ritual as *Herr Ingenieur* and *Herr Professor*, or whatever, and insist upon formal regards to the *Frau Ingenieur* and the *Frau Professor*. These encounters are check-ups on the other fellow's standing. Not to have any standing at all, to be plain old Hans or Heinrich or Wolfgang, is inconceivable.

A good many of the titles are clap-trap, even self-awarded for the sake of enhancing esteem. To hide his insignificance, a man may prefix his name on letterheads with mysterious initials, such as *Hofrat Mag. Pharm.*, or *Hofrat I.R.* or *Oberforstrat*, which, being interpreted, simply mean that he is dispensing pills behind the shop counter, or is a retired senior civil servant, or a forester.

Who is deceived? But here comes a *Präsident Arch. Prof. Dipl.-Ing.*—simply, a teacher, qualified as an architect, who is president of some society. And here comes a *Seine Spektabilität Univ.-Prof. Doktor*—in other words, the chairman of a university department. Or even a *Seine Magnifizenz Univ.-Prof.*—literally His Magnificence the University Professor. To meet a *Kammeramtsdirektor-Stellvertreter Reg.-Rat. Doktor* sounds impressive, but the chap turns out to be the deputy-director of a trade association. The litanies sound comic, but they are sung at every encounter at every moment. In January, 1978, the government decreed the abolition of 502 civil servants' titles in an attempt to bring some 20th-Century utilitarianism into the baroque hierarchy of Austrian administration, but many cherished titles have survived the purge. A diplomat, for example, may still call himself *Ausserordentlicher und Bevöllmächtigter Botschafter*, or Ambassador Extraordinary and Plenipotentiary.

An authority on this subject, Joseph Wechsberg, in his book *Sounds of Vienna*, has pointed out that a man should be addressed either by his "actual title or, if one wants to be *really* nice, by the title he would like to have, always one notch above his present title. . . . A vice-president must be addressed as '*Herr Präsident*', unless you want to offend him.

"Certain titles are subtle insults. Nearly every person wearing glasses automatically becomes a *'Doktor'*, and a bald-headed, heavy-set man is often addressed as *'Herr Direktor'*. Waiters, porters and taxi-drivers call their customers *'Herr Baron'*, generally considered a somewhat vulgar expression, or perhaps *'Exzellenz'*, if they expect a really good tip. . . . Among the Schema 1 employees of the Vienna City Administration there is a *Feldbahnfeuerlokomotivführer* (engineer-of-a-field-railway-fire-engine), a *Niederdruckheizer* (fireman-of-a-low-pressure-boiler), a *Naphthalinaufbereiter* (naphthalene dresser, whatever *he* may do)."

The harder one looks at these sublime codifications, the more placing there seems to be. The kind of house you live in, its district, the kind of job you do, all count in determining infinitesimal gradations of social esteem. It is even a matter of concern to have the lowest possible licence number

A bowler-hatted fiacre driver shelters from the drizzle as he waits for a fare. The graceful carriages, topped by facing hoods and drawn by pairs of horses, were a common mode of transport in 19th-Century Vienna. Today, perhaps 80 of the coaches are left and they are used mainly by sightseeing tourists.

for one's car. Registration plates all have a capital W, for Wien (Vienna), followed by as many as six figures. W 1 to about W 25 are reserved for the government. But the owner of W 49, say, or W 399, must by definition be a *Präsident* in his own right; he makes a point of transferring the plates from his old car to the new one.

Low numbers which people are prepared to part with are advertised in the newspapers. Once a paper did something sneaky: it ran false advertisements for a fancy low number and pretended to be holding a dutch auction with those who telephoned in to inquire about it. The point was to find out how much people were prepared to pay. The conversations were in fact recorded and the results published, amid general consternation. One bidder offered more than 100,000 schillings—over $6,000.

The disadvantage of formal behavioural codes is that they generate envy. A Viennese tends to squint over his shoulder to be sure that the other fellow is getting no more than his due. The satisfactory conclusion of his train of thought is *"Mir geht's gut"*, or "I'm all right". He reaches it thus: I am a plumber, and respected as such; but you are a lawyer, and the community tends to respect lawyers more than plumbers; I envy the extra degree of respect you have over and above me; to bridge that envy, you, the lawyer, must call me Herr Ober-Plumber, and then we shall both be able to walk away head in the air.

It works. A web of compromise is woven, and with it come certain advantages. To bring forward an example of useful compromise, there are no serious strikes in Austria because a committee, the *Paritatische Kommission* or Parities Commission, meets annually to decide what the level of wages and prices is to be, and its decision is binding. The committee is comprised of government members and representatives of both the employers and unions. It has no constitutional standing whatsoever; search the laws, and you will discover no reference to this committee. It is an open secret, an old-boy network, a meeting of friends and acquaintances, and in theory its resolutions are so much hot air. In practice they stick. The proceeding is really only the *Herr Doktor/Herr Ingenieur* business writ large. The unions and the employers are meeting on the street corner, so to speak, raising their hats and recognizing the mutual benefits of obeying the codes. And down with ideology!

Vienna's insistence on good manners is, I think, an effort to turn back the clock, as though the traumas of this century must be repressed and the older, sounder basis reconstituted. There is precious little left of the safe, ordered past except a few customs, quirks, politenesses. To reject these small mementoes of a happier time would be to opt for the emptiest modernity. As a result, hardly anyone rebels.

Back the people look to the contentments of an earlier age, to Biedermeier charms and idylls. Biedermeier was the name of a figure

Inside a cloth merchant's shop on the Albertinaplatz, a salesman examines some fabric selected from the shelves behind him. Hanging from each bale on the shelves is a white tab that specifies width, quality and price. The establishment, located just round the corner from Sacher's Hotel, is the embodiment of Viennese grand-style shopping—fit only, the decor implies, for princes and archdukes.

in some comic poems of the 1850s who was taken as the epitome of cosiness, good work, family life and prettiness at a time when these things could be enjoyed to the full. The years between the Congress of Vienna in 1815 and the revolution of 1848 are known as the Biedermeier Period. It was a unique moment of balance between progress and romanticism, between industry and poetry.

Several museums in Vienna exhibit pictures by Ferdinand Waldmüller and Moritz von Schwind, Adalbert Stifter (better known as a novelist), Rudolf von Alt and Friedrich von Amerling—all of whom painted during the Biedermeier years. What these paintings evoke is the Garden-of-Eden happiness that comes from accepting one's lot. In the Belvedere Palace hangs a conversation piece by Waldmüller—to my mind the most nostalgic of artists—and its subject is the archetypal Viennese idealization. It is entitled. "The Family of the Viennese lawyer Dr. Josef August Eltz in Ischl". (Ischl is a fashionable watering-place in the Alps where half the crowned heads of Europe used to stay; along with Baden-bei-Wien, another popular spa town, it was a pinnacle of Biedermeier aspirations.) In Waldmüller's painting, against a background of snow-capped Alps, is the entire Eltz family—Man and Nature in obvious harmony, under sunshine as bright as a blessing. To the left stands the good lawyer, correct but content, with two sons embracing him. Seated, to the right, is his wife, a baby on her lap. Another son and three older daughters are grouped helpfully about. Nothing is discordant. The Eltz family complete their own happiness, and are inviting applause for doing so.

The Biedermeier style is more than fashionable today; it is pertinent. Among the most cherished heirlooms in Vienna are portraits of ladies in ringlets, like the Eltz girls, or of grave citizens like Dr. Eltz himself. Antiques from that period—inlaid tables, bookcases, cabinets and chairs of rosewood and pear and cherry-wood—are valued for the link they provide with the idealized past, and dealers place a premium on them.

Family life in Vienna is still run according to the standards of the Biedermeier Period. As soon as possible, children are trained to obey the codes, to respect the formalities. It is astonishing how well behaved Viennese children are—or how cowed. They are seen but never heard. Even in restaurants, those grim testing-grounds of manners, tots sit moon-faced and patient.

I received a lesson in child-upbringing and code-observance when I took my three-year-old son shopping at Christmas in the Kärntnerstrasse. He spotted a toy crane as big as himself and was entranced. He wanted to play with it. At the top of his voice, he made it clear that here was his heart's delight and he exerted every trick of salesmanship on me. I spoke discouragingly about its size, its undoubted operational difficulty, its expense. I tried to shuffle the whole problem off on to Father Christmas. There broke out such a wailing that we had to leave the shop. I heard muttering about the need to give the child *"ein paar Watschen"*, a pair of slaps, which are as much a feature of Vienna as a pair of hot sausages. For a child to display temper or emotion in public could only reflect poorly on the parents. I, a grown-up with a responsibility for law and order, was visibly infringing a code: I was not punishing what ought to be punished. In fact, I returned a few minutes later to buy the crane as a Christmas present amid a circle of by-now thoroughly disapproving spectators. In their eyes, I was sparing the rod to spoil the child.

Well ordered children grow into well ordered adults. Family life in Vienna is far closer-knit than in most European or American cities. Father is still there to set a moral example; what he says, goes. Mother is in charge of the domestic economy. These days she often has a job and so is out of the house more than before; but her reign in her own field remains undisputed. Son lives at home until his student days are over, and perhaps even longer. Daughter, studying too, is a creature who would be acceptable to her long dead maidenly great-aunts. There is a Viennese word for dropout, and typically onomatopoeic it is too—*Ausgeflippter*; but there are very, very few of the miserable and emotionally wasteful tragedies that afflict England, America and Germany: children deliberately hurting their parents by maltreating themselves.

According to the Biedermeier scheme of things, there ought to be family lunch at home—mother, father, grandparents, children, as many relations as can be mustered. A big tureen of soup is served, steaming under a lid, dished out with a silver ladle, an object hallowed in a million childhood

A poodle-owner chats with a shop assistant outside a diabetics' bakery in the Naglergasse. In a city devoted to confectionery, the shop—whose advertising panels boast of five bakings a day—aims to provide an acceptable alternative for the dietetically disadvantaged.

memories; "mama" is practically synonymous with that ladle. And *Leberknödelsuppe* ought to be in the tureen, the broth with liver-dumplings that is to the Austrian soul what the heart is to the body. Then meat, then pudding. And something as substantial in the evening. The famous escalope, the *Wiener Schnitzel*, or the hardly less famous chicken *Backhändl*, both fried in breadcrumbs. Or variations on more rustic dishes: ham and eggs, potatoes, beans. No vegetable out of season.

Back in the 18th Century such heavy meals were the staple of farmhouse and cottage. Later, dressed up and served with silver ladles, they became the weekday staple of the aspiring city family. But on special occasions or when eating out, the proper meal is venison, hare, game of all kinds—food that has a special appeal because it was once eaten by those with shooting rights, in other words, only the aristocracy. In almost any Viennese restaurant nowadays, venison is singled out for its snob value and given a special place on the menu.

Another excellent place to observe class values and formalities is the Kärntnerstrasse, the moneyed backbone of Vienna—what the Bahnhofstrasse is to Zürich, the Rue du Faubourg St. Honoré to Paris, Bond Street to London. Here is the warm heart of Old Vienna. Whatever is required to delight the five senses is within walking distance. The shops are small-scale, their contents designed mostly to bolster a customer's satisfaction in his own importance: statues of Lippizaner horses to put on the dining-room table, cut-glass and crystal, porcelain, leather attaché cases, things to be wrapped in tissue paper, clothes expensively hand-tailored for men and women, fashion accessories of every kind.

To make a purchase in one of these shops is to play a comedy according to strict rules. Doors open with the ping of a bell to signal that business has started. The manager will offer effusive greetings, and a sales assistant will hurry over to ask what is wanted. A hurt expression crosses their faces if the answer is, "Nothing really, I just want to see what there is". Such frivolity, the hurt expression signifies, is simply not on for the likes of us who have counters, stocks, ledgers, carbons and triplicates. But if you state your wish, a discussion as long-winded as you please may begin.

A prolonged dialogue I once witnessed has stuck in my mind. A lady was assessing the merits of the very ordinary coat she had selected: its suitability; its brownness as opposed to its beigeness; its hem, to be lengthened or shortened. She was a tough old bird, a farmer's wife who was in Vienna for the day probably, and the salesman had become waxy-featured with perhaps 30 years of artificial indoor light. But the pair of them might have been discussing the purchase of a diadem. All in the third person. "Would the gracious lady perhaps care to consider . . . ? Would the gentleman not appreciate . . . ?" The *pas de deux* consumed almost half an hour.

No sooner is any deal clinched than the correct riposte comes, "And is there another wish?" Then the bill is made out, to be presented to a cashier at a separate till—a dragon-lady usually, business-like, with copies and rubber-stamps, making it plain that she is where the action is. After which it is permitted to return to the sales counter to collect the duly wrapped purchase, and so to proceed ceremonially to the exit, accompanied by a goodbye chorus uttered by everyone within earshot. Perhaps you bought only two pencils or a pair of shoe-laces, but you are entitled to the same elaborate reception as any splasher of cash.

To complete the mock-aristocratic illusion, enter a café. Vienna, so the boast goes, invented the coffee-house, as a result of some lucky adventurer taking possession of sacks of coffee abandoned by the Turks in the 1683 rout. (The story may even be true.) The Viennese café has as many forms as a sonata, but all share one motif: to make you feel at home without the duties of being either host or guest, to transform you into a *seigneur* waited upon by the most willing hands. Visiting in a hurry, for the sake of a guzzle, is poor form, and the disapproval will be apparent in the service. The manager or manageress should have the gravity of a butler or a housekeeper. The waitresses are so many maids, the waiters footmen. Normally they wear uniforms in the cut and colours of 1910, and they may even be assisted by *piccolos* at the bottom of the pecking-order, boys with aprons to the ground whose strings tie behind their waists. This staff provides a drawing-room ritual, no matter how many customers have to be attended to. They all serve people according to seniority, the long-established clients first, and American or Japanese tourists, I fear, last.

Visitors, on entering, may look about as though in search of friends, or they may pick and choose among the tables, many of which are likely to have reserved notices on them—a precaution against an influx that will never happen. For pastime's sake, newspapers are usually provided free, spread like great paper butterflies on a wicker frame. Read all day, if you please, self-importantly occupied, with only a *kleiner Schwarzer* or a *grosser Brauner*, Little Black and Big Brown, two characters more out of a Grimm fairy story than answering to descriptions of cups of coffee. And on the tray with the coffee will be a glass of water, and even an extra spoon to stir it with, a lordly touch. Coffee and water can be spun out indefinitely.

Come regularly enough—on two or three successive days, say—and the Herr Ober will recognize you and accept you as a steady customer. Those who keep an appointment at a fixed hour earn the right to their *Stammtisch*—their own table. After a considered period of apprenticeship, such steadies will automatically be served with what they habitually take. It is well known that at certain times of day certain people can be contacted at their *Stammtisch*. One man of the theatre has gone so far as to install a private telephone line at his table, which he treats like an office, or a salon.

Cafés as substitute homes—the places to act out extravagance, bastions of personal freedom. Is it not a proof of free will to be there at all during

Close by the Hofburg, pedestrians survey the temptations of the Kohlmarkt, an elegant shopping street named for an earlier role as the centre of trade in coal.

office hours, and to be making a series of open-ended choices? Never mind that the choices concern the taste-buds exclusively. Cake upon cake —praline, coffee, chocolate, almond, walnut, truffle; flans, tarts; cantilevered plates, or even whole pagodas of plates, with millefeuilles and pastries; flying buttresses of biscuits, baked in all shapes and as carefully piled as fine brickwork; assorted chocolates like prefab chunks of cement; the entire display having the effect of town-planning in miniature, partly zoned and partly running riot. *Schlagobers*, whipped cream, everywhere, like the newest kind of weatherproof paint. In the end, the real buildings outside come to resemble sticky puddings with meringue tops. Even the famous baroque soft ochres and yellows look like appetising sauces, the ornaments like sugar candy.

Among Vienna's cafés, the last *ancien régime* establishment is Demel, or more properly, Demel's Sohne, K.u.K. Hofzuckerbacker—Demel and Sons, Imperial-Royal Court Confectioner. Founded in 1786 by a family from Württemberg, the café took its present form in 1887, under Christoph Demel and his sons Karl and Joseph. Its entrance on the Kohlmarkt, conveniently close to the Hofburg (which it once served with ices and cakes), is unobtrusive—more than that, exclusive. A pair of swing doors with engraved glass panels open into an L-shaped room. Straight ahead is a tremendous mahogany buffet with cakes and choice snacks, canapés, duck in aspic, a spoonful of foie gras, vol-au-vents, *boeuf en croûte*, a cucumber salad—tidbits to fill a passing pang, a passing peckishness. To the right are two inter-connected rooms; in one, smoking is permitted, but hardly encouraged. Marble-topped tables, perfectly spaced to give the illusion of company without the possible inconvenience of being eavesdropped on. Period mirrors, a charming tiled floor, pretty painted plasterwork, sconces on the walls. The waitresses, wearing uniforms of black and white, address customers in the third person at its most formal.

In one of his nostalgic essays, the writer Friedrich Torberg describes how he had been a regular visitor to Demel until obliged to save his life by emigrating during the Nazi period, and how with a beating heart he then returned there after the war. It had been a 10-year gap. His usual waitress emerged through the swing doors from the kitchen, saw him but disappeared again without a greeting. He thought that he had not been recognized, but soon she returned with a confection called a "Crème Grenoble" cup, and said, "I think you haven't yet had one of these".

Whatever has been ordered at those mahogany buffets has to be fetched by these waitresses, according to a series of numbered slips as complicated as a treasure-hunt, apparently designed to show how agreeable it is to be waited on hand-and-foot. It is all very grand, but something of a charade. Demel was sold in 1972 by its last private owner, Baron Federico Berzeviczy-Pallavicini, to a Swiss finance corporation, and has been amalgamated into Vienna's largest catering service. It is directed by a swinging confectioner who, for a private party, had the Demel kitchen produce a human body made of pastry, its features finished with items like smoked salmon for skin and hard-boiled eggs for eyes, so that every bit was edible.

In the 1960s, Demel took to selling a chocolate cake generically called *Sachertorte*, a name derived from a cake originally created a century before in Sacher's Hotel. A lawsuit followed, which turned upon whether the cake of the brand-name had been baked in two sliced layers, whether it had contained a jam filling either under the chocolate icing or in the centre, and if so, what kind of jam. Sacher's Hotel had changed hands, and it was claimed by Demel that Edouard Sacher, last male of his line, had passed on the recipe to them. But Sacher's Hotel won the case, and the exclusive right to affix the "Genuine Sachertorte" seal to its cakes. The Demel cake carries its own special triangular seal to reveal its provenance. To the lay-eater, the cake in both places is similar and exquisite, but old-time experts still debate which is the more authentic.

Sacher's, a century old, commands the top of the Kärntnerstrasse, with the Opera House backing up opposite it. Frau Anna Sacher, last female of the line, smoked cigars and kept pug dogs and is remembered by the fast set of the 1920s. Incidentally, the brainless aristocrat or the chinless wonder with more money than sense was likely to haunt Sacher's, and the type was well enough known to be nicknamed Count Bobby, or in German, Graf Bobby, the butt of a steady stream of stories. Nobody is sure quite who had the genius to christen Graf Bobby—he seems to be pure folk art. After the last war, the hotel was for a time requisitioned for British officers and sank to having an army field-post number. It has again become what it was, a citadel of red plush, redolent of *chambres privées* for Graf Bobbies and ladies in thick veils.

In its hall stand potted plants and two larger-than-life marble statues of figures representing some allegory that provides a pretext to display a bare bosom. But the real point of interest in that hall is an exhibit that can serve as a kind of emblem for all that Vienna clings to: the supper menu that Crown Prince Rudolf wrote out in his own hand a few days before his suicide at Mayerling in 1889. "Oysters, turtle soup, lobster *á l'Armoricaine, truite au bleu* with Venetian sauce, quail stew, chicken *à la française*, salad, compôte, chestnut purée, ice, *Sachertorte*, cheese and fruit. With this, Chablis, Mouton-Rothschild, Röderer Champagne, Sherry Supérieure." A platonic supper, this, the ideal by which to judge others.

Congenial World of the Coffee-house

Two friends meet to sip tonic water, talk business and exchange gossip among the mahogany, brocade and marble of the Café Landtmann, near the Burgtheater.

Ever since 1683, when the Turks left behind sacks of coffee beans after their siege of Vienna and thus introduced a novel taste to the city, coffee-houses have played a central part in Viennese life. Today there are about 800 of these establishments, some of them alive with memories of an illustrious past. The Sperl, on the Lehárgasse, was a haunt of the rebel artists of the 1890s; the Café Landtmann, on the Ring, counted Sigmund Freud among its habitués; and Demel's, the café-cum-pastry shop opposite the Hofburg Palace, has been a favourite of the rich and famous for more than 150 years. Each coffee-house tends to have its faithful regulars. For the cost of a single *Mokka* (black coffee) or *Melange* (half milk, half coffee), they can spend hours chatting, reading newspapers—or simply basking in the general cosiness summed up by the word *Gemütlichkeit.*

An elderly lady uses a corner table to keep up with correspondence. Some Viennese even give their favourite café as their mailing address.

A youthful Franz Josef in his white court uniform looks out from a wall near a couple taking coffee at Demel's.

Waitresses at Demel's preside over a gourmand's dream of pastries and cakes, bearing such expressive names as Vanilla Crescents and Congress Doughnuts.

A customer lines up a shot during a game of French billiards, a form of pin pool, at the Café Sperl.

An art nouveau mirror, recalling the Café Sperl's halcyon days in the 1890s, provides a frame for a group of long-haired billiards players.

Plush upholstery, wooden reading racks, and a wide selection of newspapers and magazines make a coffee-house an ideal place for this customer to sit and read. In their enthusiasm for literature, some Viennese coffee-houses used to keep sets of encyclopaedias and even supplied house stationery to aspiring authors.

4

Life Force and Death Wish

The Berggasse, a long, straight street in the ninth district where Vienna's hospitals and medical institutes are concentrated, takes its name from the steepish slope upon which it is built. By the entrance of Number 19 is a plaque which says that the founder of psychoanalysis had lived there. Once upon a time the great man had placed his own sign right on that spot, a little black marble oblong tablet incised with gold capitals: PROF. DR. FREUD. He had lived in the apartment on the mezzanine floor, and every day he would have passed through the decorated-glass doors of this self-same parterre entrance.

In the 1960s a seamstress had occupied his rooms. But in 1971, on the initiative of Freud's devoted daughter, Anna, the specially constituted Sigmund Freud Society bought back the family apartment and opened it as a museum. Thirty-two years after his death, Freud had received his first memorial in Vienna. What other person associated with Vienna during this century has become a household name the whole world over? Yet in this city, where everyone of the most minor civic merit has been commemorated by means of statues and street names, Freud has no monument other than this museum; not so much as a cul-de-sac is named in his honour. The man who taught that the human mind will try to repress whatever is unpleasant for it to retain, has himself been repressed.

This apartment-turned-museum tells its story wonderfully. To the left of the door are the family quarters; to the right, the consulting rooms. Some of the pictures and prints—a Fuseli engraving called "The Nightmare", Ingres' picture of Oedipus and the Sphinx, prints of ladies in draperies, in the Beardsleyesque style loosely called "decadent"—might pass unnoticed had they belonged to anyone else. As Freud's, they acquire significance. And what about the antiquities he collected—grave-goods, beakers and vessels, even the skull castings of the forefathers of our species?

All around are photographs of people who had formative influences on him: Professor Carl Brühl of Vienna University, whose reading of Goethe's essay on Nature at a popular lecture had inspired Freud to study medicine; Professor von Brücke, Director of the Physiological Institute at Vienna University; Dr. Josef Breuer, also at the institute; Professor Nothnagel, a senior colleague of whom Freud was envious; Professor Charcot, foremost neurologist in Paris—great men all, but eclipsed by the strange pupil in their midst. And there in the corner, where it always was, is the couch of couches. Veneration, like syrup, has been poured over everything as a preservative.

In a sombre mood, Sigmund Freud at the age of 58 stares out of a 1914 photograph taken in his apartment at 19, Berggasse, Vienna. The war that began in August of that year brought ruination to the Austro-Hungarian Empire and convinced Freud that he had correctly diagnosed the aggressive and self-destructive impulses bedevilling mankind.

Freud's immediate friends and contemporaries, at least as shown in their photographs here, are something like a school team. Here is Nathan Weiss, from the General Hospital, who committed suicide in a public bath-house in 1883. Freud said of him: "He died from the sum total of his qualities, his pathological self-love coupled with the claims he made for the higher things of life." Near by hangs a picture of Wilhelm Fliess, the friend and colleague who helped Freud analyse himself and later quarrelled bitterly with him. Here is Stefan Zweig the writer; and here Arthur Schnitzler, the most celebrated of contemporary Viennese playwrights, to whom Freud wrote, "Whenever I get deeply absorbed in your beautiful creations, I invariably seem to find beneath their poetic surface the very presuppositions, interests and conclusions which I know to be my own. . . . Your dissection of the cultural conventions of our society, the dwelling of your thought on the polarity of love and death; all this moves me with an uncanny feeling of familiarity." Another photograph shows Otto Weininger, who took over many of Freud's ideas and became something of a cult figure for his book, *Sex and Character*. Crazed by the idea of his Jewishness, Weininger took his own life in his twenties.

The Viennese playwright Arthur Schnitzler (above) was a contemporary and friend of Freud's. Like Freud, he had trained as a doctor and he also had a gift for analysing Viennese society. He won success with comedies whose intention was to show that sexual realities make nonsense of conventional appearances.

Their Jewishness was what they had in common. The faces of the young men or the eager women whom Freud analysed are suffused with the desire to take advantage of their 19th-Century emancipation from an enclosed Jewish life and at last come to grips with the mysteries and delights of the gentile world. They produced an immense intellectual animation, a stirring and straining among received ideas. To look at the photographic records in the tiny Berggasse museum is to be swept away by a nostalgia for a Europe-that-might-have-been, a Europe where reason and progress went Onward and Upward. In the end, these rooms were ransacked by storm-troopers; the Gestapo moved in and Number 19 had a swastika over the door. On June 4, 1938, the 82-year-old Freud sought refuge in London. It had been proved to him that as a Jew he had no place in Viennese society. He had one more year to live.

What seems to be so disturbing about Freud to the Viennese is the way he came into the city from outside, absorbed the forms of its civilization, then transcended them. He had been born in Moravia, in the little town of Freiberg, called Příbor in Czech. His father was a wool merchant who had lost his livelihood in the 1850s and migrated to Vienna. Aged three, Freud became a city child, with a precious memory of a countryside where the sun shone and birds sang.

Like so many who make this kind of shift, Freud was never final about his loyalties, always testing the roots he had put down. On the one hand, he seemed the very image of the bourgeois professional man; his was a precisely measured timetable—so many hours for writing, so many more for patients, meals as the clock struck the appointed hour, a dose of exercise strolling to the *Tabaktrafik* for the cheap cigars he smoked in

Both Freud and Schnitzler worked at the Allgemeines Krankenhaus (above), Vienna's general hospital, and both met frustration in their careers. Freud had to wait years for the title of Professor, and Schnitzler lost his rank as a Reserve officer for publishing a story mocking the military concept of honour.

quantities. On the other hand, the effect of his life's work was to demolish the values he had accepted. In future, it would be impossible ever again to be an unquestioned patriarch of the sort he was himself, impossible to ask—as he did—for perfect family cohesion. It was a great contradiction. In everything he wrote, there is a feeling of turning the new leaf. In everything he did, there were conventional, even gentlemanly, inhibitions. Perhaps it was awareness of the paradox that made Freud burn all the notes and papers of his past in mid-career, simply discarding a persona.

Civilization and its Discontents, the title of one of his later books, is a splendid indication of the tensions within Freud's life in Vienna. Ambivalence like his—a desire to enjoy the capital city but to nag it to death—is a kind of human electricity specially generated in Vienna. Ernest Jones, Freud's hero-worshipping pupil from England, noted that consciously Freud loathed Vienna: "There was no beloved 'Steffel' for him, only 'that abominable steeple of St. Stefan'." Jones quoted Freud as saying, " ' If we possibly can, let us seek a home where human worth is more represented. A grave in the central cemetery is the most distressing idea I can imagine'." That approached blasphemy in this city of magnificent tombstones. Yet it was difficult to make Freud travel, and only the Nazis put an end to the lifetime he spent in Vienna, 46 years of it in the Berggasse.

Freud was expert at keeping his wounds thoroughly rubbed with salt. Inside that sombre, bearded, bourgeois moralist lurked a romantic poet, a wild man of the woods. *The Psychopathology of Everyday Life*, one of his most influential books, gives away Freud's longing to reduce his inner chaos to order. In the most trivial social routines and undignified details of bodily functions, he tried to find meaning and even scientific truths. A man stumbling on a doorstep, for instance, is not the victim of an accident; he is expressing the prone-to-stumbling compulsion within him. From this view springs the vulgar idea that nobody is ill without wanting to be. But there were, in fact, no consistent systems of this kind, no such psychopathology of everyday life. Illusory explanations for human behaviour of all kinds were pouring out of Freud's imagination, but these explanations were based upon Viennese trivialities of place and culture, stratifications, personal inconsequences. There was nothing universal or solid enough in such glorified generalizations to be called scientific.

His theories spring straight from the environment. The "pleasure principle" and "pain principle"—what better reflections could there be of the positive and negative aspects of living in Vienna? The "life force" in conflict with the "death wish"—what is that but a caricature of the empire as it struggled with its own decadence? His linking of creative output with physical evacuation of the bowels arose from the all-important problem of indigestion in a city given to over-eating. His identification of totems and taboos was specially apposite. Vienna was, and is, alive with taboos. The entire society was regulated, consciously and unconsciously, by awareness of what was done and what was not done. Daily life, clothing, manners, upbringing, forms of address, were hedged about with taboos. The whole class structure was one mammoth taboo. Nor was Freud quite so free from the self-deceptions that accompany taboos as he liked to suppose. The writer Arthur Koestler has recalled an interview in 1938 in which Freud spoke about the cancer which had afflicted him since 1923, but which taboo prevented him from calling more than "this thing on my lip".

There could have been no better a totem than the Emperor Franz Josef, under whose reign Freud spent his formative years. Friedrich Heer, professor of history at Vienna University, has shown in a brilliant essay about Freud "how closely his concept of a hierarchy within the personality was modelled on the complicated orders within the Habsburg monarchy. . . . Life, the personality, had to carry the troublesome burden of the id. As the personification of unbridled pleasure (Freud was a puritan) it needed the stabilizing power of a realistic principle to keep it in check: the ego. The ego bore a heavy responsibility, like all politicians in the non-Hungarian half of the Empire. The ego had to be the buffer between the blind urges of the populace, of the id, and the wearisome external realities of life in those days, from 1866 to 1914! The ego had to mediate between the ever-rebellious lower regions, the id, and the above stairs of super-ego. . . . The super-ego is like Franz Josef, but even surpasses and transcends him."

Freud was fascinated by superstition, of which there was plenty for him to observe in Vienna. Holy charms—Catholic medallions, crucifixes, silver images of the Virgin—still hang in all sorts of places in Vienna, from car

Freud was 80, and just three years from death, when he sat for this 1936 photograph in his cluttered Berggasse study. With him is his pet chow, Jo-fi.

In the Inner City's Bäckerstrasse, a woman keeps watch on the world from an upper window of a house decorated with a shrine to the Virgin Mary. Today, as in Freud's time, the streets of Vienna contain many reminders of the city's prevailing Catholic faith—the basis for his theories about the power of "totem and taboo".

windows to key-chains. A framed photograph of husband or wife or child will commonly have an image of the Virgin Mary or some saint dangling from a top corner as though on permanent guard. The insistence on framed photographs itself has something to do with the properties of preservative magic. Every living-room table is a clutter of tent-like frames. The Kärntnerstrasse abounds in shops selling fabulous frames of silver, lapis lazuli, amber, onyx and agate, as though the precious stones or metals had some correspondence to the loved one captured inside.

Not all charms are holy. Girls wear bracelets a-jangle with gold representations of chimney sweeps, four-leaf clover and red-capped white-spotted mushrooms—all of which are thought to bring good luck. The trinkets come in candy form too, for eating at Christmas or on New Year's Eve. And, of course, the real thing is thought to be most efficacious of all. If people are sitting on grass—picnicking, say—they are likely to search instinctively for four-leaf clover. The plants are also cultivated and sold in small pots.

Freud's fascination with superstition stemmed from his belief in the ineradicable, unregenerate primitiveness of man. He studied jokes for what they revealed of the primitive man. Word-play and puns, the staple of the Viennese cabaret, were, he realized, oblique insights into personality. He conceived of personality as an accumulation of unconscious memories, inherited lore, tribal wisdom and unwisdom. In his view, people were unable to shake free from the scraps of the past and were virtually incapable of reaching up to positive virtues and values. He advocated that people should confront their traumas, but held out little hope of consolation from doing so. To perceive fully the causes of unhappiness did not lead to overcoming them, but to resignation. His was a wholly realistic pessimism, in total conformity to the Vienna in which he lived. His work turned round the philosophy, sung in Johann Strauss's Operetta *Die Fledermaus*: "Happy is the man who forgets what he cannot change." It was what had been forgotten that interested Freud, and the morbid touch in this explains why Freud was and is treated like an outcast at home. The Viennese, especially, would go off their heads if they concentrated upon truthfully remembering, instead of selectively forgetting, their past.

Dreams. A thousand books rhapsodize about Vienna as a city of dreams. Everybody knows popular songs like *Wien, Stadt meine Traüme*— "Vienna, City of my Dreams". Freud held that dreams have multiple meanings, being fundamentally representations of latent hopes or fears, translating into images or language what the unconscious mind knows but conceals. In *The Interpretation of Dreams* Freud did a certain amount of self-analysis, delving into his relationship with his father and his memories of the lost countryside of his youth. Freud's unpopularity began there, for the process of analysis brings the Viennese hard up against their wilfully sentimental portrait of themselves, but it was sealed by his exposé of something very similar—the Viennese hypocrisy about sex.

When he called the mouth "the oral sexual organ" or suggested that the nose had "a genital formation", he was awakening people out of a dream and drawing their attention to a reality—an unusual reality and one that violated canons of contemporary good taste; but once said, these things could not be retracted. Wasn't it easier to write Freud off as a charlatan? Wasn't he laughing at them? "I am also getting used to regarding every sexual act as one between four individuals," he declared in a letter to Wilhelm Fliess. What could have been in Prof. Dr. Freud's mind, I wonder, to write a thing like that? Really!

Freud's outspokenness put a brake on his career. He had received his medical degree in 1881 and in the following year joined the staff of the great teaching hospital, the Allgemeines Krankenhaus. He was appointed lecturer in 1885, the year before he set up his practice as a psychoanalyst. Not until 1902, when he was 46, did he receive a letter from the Minister of Education announcing that he had been awarded the title of Professor. The delay of his appointment, even if it had been only a matter of bureaucracy, had been scandalous. As Freud commented to Wilhelm Fliess, "Congratulations and bouquets keep pouring in, as if the role of sexuality had been suddenly recognized by His Majesty, the interpretation of dreams confirmed by the Council of Ministers, and the necessity of the psychoanalytic therapy of hysteria carried by a two-thirds majority in Parliament."

The trouble about Freud's views on sexuality was that most people felt he was right, and also felt guilty about it. Sex—except between lawful husband and wife—was so hedged in with taboo that people were either ashamed of themselves or frustrated. To seduce a woman was shameful; not to seduce her, however, was masculine impotence. Appetite, in the Germanic scheme of things, meant performance—the sexual urge was there to be gratified. But the Italianate side of life in Vienna was flirtatious: seduction, though also hopefully consummated, was first and foremost artistic. In either case, never mind what was really said or done, Viennese custom allowed men but not women to indulge themselves, and in that double standard was a sexual labyrinth. Mozart's Don Giovanni tots up the numbers of his female conquests with brutal nonchalance, but the ladies of that opera—and of *Figaro*, too—are heartshaken by a mere token of love. How high-flown these feminine sentiments are, how earthy is masculine fun! Whom did Don Giovanni and his kind conquer? The answer is *demi-mondaines*, kept women, actresses and dancers, washerwomen, cocottes.

Stefan Zweig, who wrote about Freud and even gave an oration at his funeral in London, described the taboos very well in the *World of Yesterday*, his autobiography, and one of the last books he wrote before putting an end to his life of exile in Brazil. The atmosphere in which he and his Viennese contemporaries grew up, he says, was "sticky, perfumed, sultry, unhealthy. . . . This dishonest and unpsychological morality of secrecy and hiding hung over us like a nightmare. . . . Everywhere the suppressed sought byways, loopholes and detours." Far from creating a moral climate, repression spawned pornography, hysteria, fantasies.

Hypocrisy grew into the order of the day. Thousands of prostitutes—"a gigantic army" in Zweig's phrase—were on the streets, yet when emancipated girls first rode bicycles, the city professed to be shocked. The red-light district in the Rotenturmstrasse was in the shadow of the cathedral (where it still is today, much reduced). "Only a very few particularly rich young men could afford the luxury of keeping a mistress, that is, taking an apartment and paying her expenses," writes Stefan Zweig. "And only a very few fortunate young men achieved the literary ideal of love of the times—the only one it was permitted to describe in novels—an affair with a married woman. The others helped themselves for the most part with shopgirls and waitresses. . . . It was only the girls of the very poorest proletarian background who were sufficiently unresisting on the one hand, and had enough freedom on the other, for such passing relationships without serious thoughts of marriage." The sidewalks, he says, were so sprinkled with women for sale that it was impossible to avoid them. "The official attitude of the State and its morality towards this shady affair was never a very comfortable one. . . . A distinction was made between private prostitution, which the State prosecuted as immoral and dangerous, and legalised prostitution which it supplied with a sort of trade licence and which it taxed."

No sexual adventure could have had an unhappier ending than the Crown Prince Rudolf's love for his young mistress Marie Vetsera. The

On a bench in the Stadtpark, a woman smiles indulgently as a boy and girl embrace beside her. In Freud's home city, as in other cities of the Western world, psychoanalytic theories helped open the way to a less repressive and less guilt-ridden attitude towards sex.

tragedy of the lovers' mutual suicide was a glimpse into the obvious. It was plain to everybody that the most exalted personages in the land were really up to the same affairs as everybody else. The imperial court had the true 19th-Century instinct to hush it up. This was impossible, and the truth soon got out; but the Crown Prince was buried in state, with full religious rites, as though he had not died by his own hand. It was kinder to fudge.

Codes of make-believe also spread to homosexuality. Many more of those severe, monocled *k. und k.* officers were homosexual than cared to admit it. With their touchiness about honour, and their military rigidity, they were a particularly repressed caste. There again, a glimpse of the truth was to be had in the summer of 1913. Colonel Redl, a general staff officer, was found to have betrayed military plans to the Russians in order to pay off those who were blackmailing him as a homosexual. General Conrad von Hötzendorf, Chief of General Staff, had "to save the Army from worse dishonour", and Redl was put under arrest in a hotel, with two fellow-officers to stand guard over him while he blew out his brains.

The important commandment to obey was the eleventh, Thou Shalt Not Be Caught. Imagine the response when a semi-medical, semi-prophetic voice from the Berggasse invites—commands—the public to analyse sexual behaviour and its implications. Who wants to have their noses rubbed in their own hypocrisy? When one mother wrote in distress to beseech him to cure her son of his homosexuality, Freud curtly told her that it was not a disease, and that many of the world's great men had been homosexuals. Such a line of argument would never have saved Colonel Redl from paying the price.

I sometimes wonder how Freud got away with so much. He certainly enjoyed sailing close to the wind, and did so with the illusion that he was always right. He was allowed to carry on, I believe, because he was in a city where men of letters were tolerated, even encouraged, so long as they stuck to their circle. His publications were regarded less as scientific studies than as avant-garde literature. Another twist of sensationalism, and he could have been a scribbler in a café. His case-notes about Dora, the Rat Man, Anna O, Elizabeth von R and others are absolute short stories; the abbreviated names of his patients sound like names in a tale by Kleist or Goethe. His interpretations of the lives of Leonardo, Moses and Oedipus are pure historical novels. Wasn't there hiding behind that clipped beard and glasses and the name which simply means "joy" just another Jewish *boulevardier* who could not decide whether his fate was tragic or comic?

Dora and Anna O might also have been characters invented by Arthur Schnitzler, the playwright for whom Freud had confessed his "uncanny feeling of familiarity". In his autobiography, *My Youth in Vienna*, Schnitzler gives a marvellously carefree description of his time as a "roué on a shoe-string". Fännchen, Helene, Anni, Toni, Charlotte, Gisela, Olga, Jeanette—the girls combine into a type he called *süsses Mädel*, "a sweet girl". He takes them for walks to the Prater, for excursions into the Wienerwald, and to open-air cafés; they flutter in his arms; he seduces them. He has no regrets, but then he was armoured by the artist's chilling knowledge that he was getting material to write about.

Schnitzler was the son of a well-known physician, and himself became a doctor. He practised at the Allgemeines Krankenhaus, as Freud had done, and turned his observations into eroticism, depicted in a light and cynical prose. *Reigen*, written in 1900, was his best known play because a far-fetched version of it called *La Ronde* was filmed half a century later. In this work, sex makes the world go round: prostitute meets soldier, soldier meets maid, maid meets man-about-town, man-about-town meets married lady; husband meets *süsses Mädel, süsses Mädel* meets poet, poet meets actress; actress meets count, count meets prostitute. It doesn't seem too much to say that Schnitzler, like Freud, was reporting case histories, but whereas the former put a satirical gloss on his reportage, the latter made heavier generalizations.

Schnitzler and Freud also had in common the social layers that they explored. Neither was much concerned with the proletariat invisibly crowded away outside the city centre. Freud's patients were well-off. Schnitzler observed the upper bourgeoisie and minor nobility—doctors, officers, younger sons, Jewish intellectuals and businessmen. An aura of allure surrounded their subjects, who were flattered by Schnitzler's attentions, glamorizations even. To that extent, he was helping to create the myth of "gay Vienna". In fact his approach, like Freud's, is negative

Crown Prince Rudolf shocked the Austro-Hungarian Empire in 1889 when he shot himself and his 18-year-old mistress Marie Vetsera (far right) at Mayerling, the imperial hunting-lodge 22 miles from Vienna. In Freudian terminology, the lovers were expressing the "death wish", a primary human instinct that often prompts people to act against their own best interests.

beyond retrieve. Both men considered that humanity was bound to fall short of its ideals. Not only was human activity predictably conditioned by parents and childhood, but always with negative results. It was easy to turn everything inside out. Positive virtues were explained away by being stood on their head. Heroism was simply foolishness or failure to recognize danger; generosity was a form of meanness, in that the donor put the recipient in his debt; love was an expression of egoism. These theorems were infinitely amusing in the Vienna cafés of the day, but hardly encompass the whole human personality.

Sometimes Schnitzler's techniques even seem like Freud's. One of his stories, usually accepted as a masterpiece, is *Leutnant Gustl*, published in 1901. A monologue, it might be some rush of words for Freud to report from his consulting-room couch. A little lieutenant at a concert has had a row with an acquaintance in the cloakroom, a master-baker, nouveau riche, who dares lay hands on the officer's sword, the very emblem of his superiority. The master-baker ought to be punished, but the officer has neither the presence of mind nor the courage to do it. If word gets out, the lieutenant will be dishonoured, may even be arraigned before a tribunal of scornful brother officers and stripped of his rank. His only way out is to shoot himself, which he prepares to do, in the very manner to be adopted by the unfortunate Colonel Redl. At the last moment he hears that the master-baker has died of a timely stroke. The lieutenant's skin is saved. But, says Schnitzler, he never had any honour to lose in the first place.

Publishing this story, Schnitzler aroused the kind of scandal that Freud did. He too was asking questions about hypocrisy. He had cut too close to the bone. He was deprived of his rank as a Reserve officer.

One topic Schnitzler touched on with forced frivolity was syphilis. It was no joke. The cure was painful and humiliating. Syphilis was to the end of the last century what cholera had been to its beginning. And one person at least, Hitler, had been terrified by it. Through *Mein Kampf* throbs a crazy obsession with syphilis as a disease carried in the wake of

Jews and Bolsheviks. Hitler's dread of syphilis was so rabid that some commentators have thought he must have caught it in his days in the Vienna slums. There is a correspondence between the brilliant neuroticisms of Schnitzler and Freud, and Hitler's view of the world. The responses may look opposed superficially, but they are part and parcel of the tangle of guilts and repressions in which the poor 20th Century was born.

In the essay I have already mentioned, Professor Friedrich Heer, referring to the Nazism ahead, makes this terrible but profound judgment on the Viennese society in which Freud worked: "They were suicides about to become murderers." It is impossible not to observe how many suicides there were in Freud's circle, carried out on the spur of the moment, as often as not, while the balance of mind was certainly disturbed. It is as though these men suddenly wearied of the burden of being themselves. The chase after prostitutes, risking the prevalent syphilis, was courting death by a longer route than the one offered by a revolver bullet, but it was suicidal in its way. And in Schnitzler's stories, too, death is ever-present—either by suicide, or duelling, which is tantamount to the same thing, for it was to stake one's life on hazard.

So much gaiety, so much self-obliteration. Professor Heer is right. The aggression that was turned against the self would be expressed against others, the moment circumstances permitted. Nazism, inspiring the huge majority of Austrians, released or externalized these inner aggressions. And it was collective suicide as well, in that these people, as Nazis, broke the age-old taboos about the shedding of human life—thereby challenging the rest of the world to impose upon them the supreme penalty. Freud's formulation of the death wish as one of the great driving engines of humanity is a true insight into the spirit of the time and place.

Pick up any Viennese newspaper today, and sad stories of self-destruction leap off the page. Here is a young professor, with apparently everything to look forward to, who has cut his throat. Here is a 22-year-old worker in a factory who has shot himself without warning in the lavatory during a break. Some of the chosen means of suicide have about them a touch that seems deliberately, pointedly, macabre. A dentist strangles himself on the electric flex of his drill; a peasant drowns himself in a vat of his cider; a housewife meticulously scrubs her kitchen and then blows her head off in it.

Vienna has a suicide rate of about 25 to each 100,000 citizens, the highest in Austria. Austria itself has a rate of 22 suicides per 100,000, which places it above such countries as Sweden and Finland, for all their well-publicized Nordic gloom. Only Hungary, at 29 per 100,000, has a more unenviable record on this chart, and that may reflect some hangover from the Austro-Hungarian past. A suicide rate like Vienna's must express a fundamental inner malaise; the symptom is not in doubt, but the causes given are various. Some sociologists say that the young are particularly at risk because they do not have a sense of purpose in their careers. Others maintain that the breakdown of the family has created lonelinesses which people cannot cope with; too many are living alone, without means of making worthwhile contacts with others.

Professor Erwin Ringel of Vienna University is a world authority on suicide. I visited him at his office in the Allgemeines Krankenhaus, greatly modernized since Freud worked there. In the psychiatric department where Professor Ringel works, visitors and patients and staff wander about in an open-plan architecture; the layout may be in accordance with latest theories, for all I know, but it creates the impression of a traditional bedlam where the healthy amuse themselves by coming to gawp at the sick. In his office are a large and well-carved statue of the Virgin, and also an encyclopaedia of Catholic morals.

"People don't communicate," Professor Ringel says. "It's a special irony, since we are supposed to be so *Gemütlich*, so cosy and charming. We reach the limits of *Gemütlichkeit* and find there is nothing to it, so the disappointment is all the greater. For many suicides the decisive point comes in early childhood. They have been given a view of self-doubt, they feel themselves hindered or handicapped, and lose the joy of life. Suicide, as Freud shows, has to do with aggression. So many of us are traumatized, and have nowhere to turn but inwards. The potential for aggression cannot be brought out here in Vienna. It's a civilized place, and in our civilization it becomes more and more difficult to canalize aggression, and so people use it against themselves.

"In the Sixties, the rate of suicide was over 30 per 100,000, so it's going down, but suicide has to do with unconquered emotion, and that's Viennese. You know, we did a comparative study of suicide in Vienna and Los Angeles. Over there, so we found, people said, 'What a pity, think of all he could have contributed to the community'. And here, the attitude was, 'Good for him, he's got it over with, he's all right'.

"There is some close relationship here with death. Look at our *Heurigen* songs, the songs that celebrate the first wine of the season. *Verkauft's mei G'wand, I Fahr in Himmel*, 'Sell my old clothes, I'm off to Heaven'. *Es wird ein Wein sein, und wir werdn nimmer sein*, 'There'll be wine and we won't be here for it'. *Zehn Schilling für die Schrammelmusik und in der Früh gehn ma Sterben,* 'Ten schillings for the folk-music and in the morning we'll croak'—what a couplet that is! The music warns us not to wait. These songs have a dark death wish, as Freud described it."

5

Variations on a Musical Theme

Vienna is associated, rightly and wrongly, with a great musical tradition. Rightly, because many of the great classical composers lived and worked in the city. Gluck, Haydn, Mozart, Beethoven and Schubert were all composing in Vienna within a span of 50 years, from about 1780 to 1830. Brahms, Bruckner, Mahler, Hugo Wolf and Johann Strauss were there in the late 19th Century. The creators of 20th-Century classical music—Schoenberg, Berg and Webern—followed them. The roll-call of honour is long and all very impressive; and it is very much a cause for Viennese pride today that such a large proportion of Western classical music was written by men with whom they can claim special familiarity. But is Vienna still the capital of serious music? Is it in the forefront of musical creativity? That is where the reputation becomes debatable.

The official view—and it is very official, because the musical bureaucracy formed during the Habsburg years has been preserved under the Ministry of Culture and Education, complete with a chancellery, ministers and secretaries of state—is that great music springs from the soil of Austria. A divine gift for music supposedly pervades the landscape, the people, the atmosphere, and even saturates the stones of Vienna. Propaganda of this kind knows no bounds. The civil servants who perpetrate it would have everybody believe that Mozart and Beethoven represent the Viennese spirit, and nothing but the Viennese spirit. The great composers are venerated less for their genius than for the accident of where they once lived. Their historical presence seems to reassure every inhabitant of Vienna that he shares in something glorious and universal. Just to hear the opening bars of Mozart's "Jupiter" symphony, say, or Beethoven's Fifth, is enough to make even the most unmusical Viennese feel thoroughly self-satisfied.

It is natural for the Viennese to assume that this tradition could not possibly fade, although it is a matter of observance that for 50 years now Vienna has produced neither composers nor musicians who can possibly rank with the past. There ought to have been a grand revival after the Second World War, but it has not taken place. State initiatives, such as Austria's Intellectual Life scheme, which sponsors recordings of works by 20th-Century Austrian composers, have still to make headway.

The old and tried continue to have their appeal. The transistor and rock-and-roll revolution may have come, but not at the expense of the classical favourites. In this city, musical life still goes on much as it did around the 1870s. The chief musical institutions of those days are all

Opera-goers in evening dress pass down the grand staircase of the Vienna State Opera House, which numbers the composers Gustav Mahler and Richard Strauss among its past directors. In the eyes of Austria's musical establishment the State Opera ranks as the centrepiece of national culture.

kept alive and in trim: the State Opera, known simply as the Opera; the second opera house, the Volksoper, for operettas; the famous Vienna Philharmonic Orchestra; the influential Gesellschaft der Musikfreunde, or Society of Friends of Music, which has commissioned much new work in the past and has counted Schubert and Beethoven among its members and Brahms among its directors; the Vienna Boys Choir, which each week sings Mass in the Hofburg Chapel.

The opening bars of the popular classics may well be fixed in most Viennese heads, but not so firmly nor so affectionately as the one truly indigenous musical form: the waltz. For more than a hundred years now, the waltz has set the city's musical tone. Nobody suggests it is first-rate music, but the whole world recognizes it as Vienna's signature tune.

The waltz tempo developed in the early 19th Century out of *Ländler*—Austrian peasant dances that were ideal for conveying simple emotions simply. The contrast with the controlled and formal minuet—the 18th-Century step *par excellence*—is absolute. The waltz is libido free as air; it is programme music for the senses, a form of musical journalism to describe the emotions. On occasion it is literal programme music, punctuated with the sounds of sleigh bells, hammers, the crack of whips—anything appropriate to the theme. The best waltzes have moods; they put across themes of longing and love, of joy and misery and frustration, quick-changing cloudbursts of temperament corresponding to our own under-the-skin sensations. Like a poem, a Viennese waltz tells us what we know about ourselves but have not yet expressed.

In 1832, the 19-year-old Richard Wagner visited Vienna from Germany. He too, like the greatest waltz composers, had the gift of extracting the loose material of the subconscious and putting it into his own musical form, in his case often sinister. He had this to say of the waltz as it swept Vienna for the first time—like a drug, he thought, more powerful than alcohol: "I shall never forget the extraordinary performance of Johann Strauss, who put equal enthusiasm into everything he played, and very often made the audience almost frantic with delight. At the beginning of a new waltz this demon of the Viennese musical spirit shook like a Pythian priestess on the tripod, and veritable groans of ecstasy (which, without doubt were more due to his music than to the drinks in which the audience had indulged) raised their worship for the magic violinist to almost bewildering heights of frenzy."

The violinist was Johann Strauss the Elder, who played while simultaneously conducting his ensemble. Perhaps this personal panache was part of his success, too. Certainly there was no holding the waltz craze. The romantic movement in European arts and letters was in full bloom; passion and moonlight and Gothic ruins were replacing reason and clear skies and Greek temples. Whereas the rest of Europe had visions of pale maidens wandering deserted on cliff-tops and young men blowing out

In a scene from a Viennese production of the operetta "The Beggar Student", the hero triumphantly exposes the cringing villain. With its white-gloved intrigue and happy ending, the operetta has enjoyed high regard in Vienna—home of the composer, Carl Millöcker—ever since it was first staged there in 1882.

their brains because the extravagance of their passions was too much for them, the Viennese contributed a dance in which everyone could join. *Fasching*, the carnival season between Christmas and Lent, became a festival of waltzing, and so it has remained ever since.

Johann Strauss the Elder was a nonconformist as well as a celebrity. In 1844, he left the wife with whom he had had six children in order to run off with a milliner, with whom he had five. By then, he was being challenged by his son, Johann Strauss the Younger. Two other sons also wrote successful waltzes. The elder Strauss must have felt that the rivalry of his brood was cutting away the ground under his feet. He was frightened by the 1848 revolution, that upsurge of the young, and he died the year after. The way was then open for Johann Strauss the Younger to capture Vienna as no other musician has ever done.

The economic boom early in Franz Josef's reign had created new middle classes excited by the vista of their future. Money and social success were there for the having. Vienna, source of good things, needed celebrating. There was a deep-held tradition of popular songs in praise of Vienna and its virtues which led in the end to such immortal feelings as: "*Es gibt nur a Kaiserstadt, es gibt nur a Wien* (There's only one imperial city, there's only one Vienna)"; "*Wien, Wien, nur du allein* (Vienna, Vienna, you alone)." Vienna thought of itself as the city of dreams that come true. Nature, too, needed celebrating. Strauss's musical sequence *Tales from the Vienna Woods* and *The Blue Danube* are supreme romanticisms of place, declarations of love for a capital as well as for its surroundings.

No occasion was complete without a statement from Strauss. Everyone wanted to commission something from him, and he usually accepted, rushing to get the notes down at the eleventh hour, scoring them at full speed—waltzes, and polkas and marches, too. He composed nearly 500 works in all. Two hundred copyists were at his command. He stayed up all night busily scratching away with a steel pen. He undertook semi-regal tours abroad, to England, to America, and to Russia; he became an unmatched Viennese institution.

After his first successes, he turned to operettas, a genre for which he thought himself specially gifted. An operetta could enlarge the scope of the more momentary or fleeting waltz. The mood of his music could now be expressed by stories on a stage. *Die Fledermaus*, his masterpiece, which was composed in 43 days, was a comment on the times. The operetta was first performed on April 5, 1874. That was eight years after the shattering Austrian defeat by Prussia at Königgrätz, and one year after "Black Friday", when the Vienna Stock Exchange collapsed after years of boom. Strauss may have averted his eyes from that reality. But he was not unaware of it, as the well-known words from *Fledermaus*, "Happy is the man who forgets what he cannot change", bear witness. Indeed, several writers have pointed out that the words might well serve as a motto for Vienna.

According to the operetta ideal, true love exists, all the better for having to survive a nice little obstacle course. In the end, everything has to turn out for the best. Mozart had already staged the most perfect operatic finale, in *Figaro*, when the couples are united and singing in unison, *"Gloria Tutti"*—in other words, Here's to Everyone. Strauss added in his laughter and champagne and pretty girls. Where 19th-Century philosophers argued about the inevitable progress of man, he and the other Austrian operetta composers urged it in song: Franz von Suppé, who wrote *Boccaccio*; Karl Zeller and *The Bird Catcher*; Millöcker with his *The Beggar Student*; Emmerich Kálmán with *Gräfin Mariza*; Carl Michael Ziehrer and his *Viennese Children*; Robert Stolz and *The Lost Waltz*; Franz Lehár, who wrote *The Merry Widow*, the operetta that has enjoyed greater worldwide success than any other. All these men stand together in the sunlight of a brief moment when it was possible, normal even, to raise a voice on behalf of the happy ending.

Once I was fortunate enough to meet Robert Stolz, 89 years old at the time and near the end of his life. His operetta songs had been a huge success on both stage and screen, but Stolz was conscious that he was the last of the heady line of operetta maestros and that the genre was nearly played out. I was astonished to hear from him that, in 1905, he had conducted the first performance of *The Merry Widow*. He remembered Lehár well, and described how the composer would take a table in a fashionable café and sit writing his scores in full view of everybody,

Johann Strauss the Younger, the waltz king of Vienna, is lampooned as a gypsy violinist in a cartoon from an Austrian satirical magazine of 1883. In the course of a 50-year career that produced some 400 memorable waltzes, he eclipsed the success of his father and namesake, the first great popularizer of the dance.

glowering, as if daring his friends to approach him. In the end Lehár turned Nazi, but by then gaiety had had its day.

Operetta could not hold its own in the Jazz Twenties and the storm-cloud Thirties. In no time at all, the Austrian Nazis were rooting about in Johann Strauss's ancestry, falsifying the certificate of his great-grand-parents' marriage, which showed him to be of Jewish origins; they could not possibly admit that the man who had captured the Viennese soul had not possessed the right racial qualifications. After the Nazi period, conditions were unfavourable to the writing of new operettas, but the old favourites were as much in demand as ever. When I visited Vienna in 1955, American music was played only in one nightclub, but there was a choice of several operettas in the theatres. Even now the Volksoper repertoire always includes *The Merry Widow*, as well as *Fledermaus*. The Volksoper is not just a museum where period pieces are trotted out; it is integral to the well-being of Vienna, a clinic where moral and mental equilibrium is toned up. On the smiling faces of the Volksoper audiences is to be seen the longing for a happy ending after all.

Waltzing, also, has been proof against the times. It is a dance that Viennese of all generations have in common, and they know they are doing it—in setting, style and rhythm—as it was always done. What keeps the waltz alive as the queen of traditional dances is *Fasching*, carnival time. It may not be what it once was, not even the annual fête it is in Munich, but it provides a marvellous opportunity to demonstrate a grasp of etiquette and social distinctions.

Once, in the Middle Ages, *Fasching* was a bacchanalia. Even in Strauss's day, people used to let their hair down, dancing night after night until dawn. But since then it has been becoming ever more genteel and now the waltzers seize the opportunity to show exactly what their station is in society. For each trade or professional body or association, there is a *Fasching* ball with the appropriate degree of grandeur. No group wants to be out of the swim. Every night of the week between mid-January and mid-February there is at least one ball, often several, with a dozen on Fridays and Saturdays. There is a ball for the Trade Union of Post Office Employees, Grades 16 and 17; there is another for the ÖAAB-Landesberufssektion, Öffentlicher Dienst, in other words the conservative party's association of workers and employees, civil service section; there is a *Zuckerbäckerball* for confectioners, and a Bonbon-Ball for the Central Association of Sweet Wholesalers and Retailers. There are balls for the city gardeners, for the gas and waterpipe repairmen, for the Croats of the Burgenland, for the Czech Catholics in Vienna; a ball for this factory and that bank, for a district, a freemasonry, a club, the old boys of a school. There is even a fancy dress ball—a *Gschnasball*, or *Gschnas*, for short. Children are also catered for; they, too, can enjoy

A violinist accompanies his work with a good-humoured smile at the dancers.

Glittering Rituals of the Ballroom

One of the highlights of the Viennese calendar is the Press Club's Concordia Ball, held every June in the Town Hall. Like all major balls in Vienna, the Concordia has its own set of rituals and a body to watch over them: the "honourable committee", which supervises details ranging from floral arrangements to the choice of dancers to perform the opening polonaise.

While their escorts bow discreetly, girls in long white dresses and elbow-length gloves curtsey to the committee that selected them to start the dancing.

Beneath a double row of chandeliers, a multi-coloured throng of dancers fills the floor of the Vienna Town Hall's enormous, neo-Gothic banqueting chamber.

such specialities as the *Kinderfaschingsfest* of the Private Schools for Lutherans. Even those who disapprove of the whole thing will probably go to the *Jägerball*, theoretically for huntsmen but in practice an informal, bohemian affair at which people wear whatever costume they wish.

The *Jägerball* takes place in the Sofiensale, a former indoor public swimming pool with rustic frescos. For the majority of the balls—especially the grandest, the so-called noble balls—the former palaces once again come into their own. Their great rooms are hired out by their present owners—the state, big insurance companies, and the like—and the ceremonies of the past can be imitated in the correct surroundings.

The most prestigious ball, much trumpeted in the Press, takes place at the Opera. A dance floor is laid over the seats in the stalls, the boxes are reserved, and the Vienna Philharmonic Orchestra obliges, usually under the baton of some famous conductor who must look as if he is putting his all into Strauss's *Wiener Blut* waltzes or the *Tric-Trac Polka.* Debutantes make their grand entry, 30 or 40 of them—girls from families with titles, what is more, in this republic where a title is as visible as a halo around a forehead. The girls have been vetted, according to custom, by a dragon of a countess who has an eye for coats of arms and pedigrees; and woe betide, shall we say, the *Zuckerbäcker's* daughter who tries to slip through the net. She will be firmly kept in her station.

Young men from the best families are the escorts. They wear white tie—*frack* as the Viennese call it—and the girls wear long white dresses. There's a tailor, Lambert Hofer, which hires out the full *frack* kit, and you can spoil a man's evening by hissing in his ear what you can spot a mile off by its cut, "Lambert Hofer!" In theory, tickets for all the noble balls are readily for sale, and any Tom, Dick or Harry can buy his way in and go in hired *frack.* But he would be unwise to try it.

Manners for evenings like these do not come naturally. Dancing masters exist to school the young of the middle and upper classes, the way Lippizaner horses are put through dressage. Elmayer's! The name will spark off childhood memories for every Viennese with a well-ordered past. Colonel Willy von Vestenbrugg-Elmayer belonged to the old guard. He wore a monocle. He ran a dancing school in rooms by the side of the Palais Pallavicini, which faces the Hofburg, and there he taught the waltz as it was supposed to be danced. He had lost a leg in the First World War, but that did not render him unfit to be a dancing master. He had instructors to demonstrate the steps, which left him free to concentrate on his chief concern: codes of conduct. How to leave a visiting card, how to call on the parents of girls one hoped to invite to a ball, how to introduce people correctly—on such matters, his views were of the strictest sort, long after the world to which this all belonged had foundered, and nobody any longer knew or really cared what the colonel was talking about.

Colonel Elmayer died in the 1960s, and although his dancing school is still going, it has a rival now—the school of Professor Willy Fränzl. In his day Willy Fränzl was a ballet dancer; the title of professor is purely honorific, to lend prestige to his enterprise. His school is neatly located behind the Eislaufverein, the Ice Skating Association, where the music of the outdoor skating rink can just be heard. I went to the school one evening, to find some 20 earnest teenagers nervously gyrating to recordings of waltzes. The young men wore white gloves, and they were sweating with nervous strain. Professor Fränzl had already hurried away to a *Tanzprobe*, a dance rehearsal for a ball. He was apparently in the Hofburg Palace itself. Intrigued, I tracked him down there and became caught up in the preparations for the *Ball der Pharmazie*, also called the *Apothekenball*—the chemists' and druggists' annual *Fasching* jamboree.

There, in one of the huge marble rooms of the former imperial court, the professor stood on a platform struggling with an apparently insuperable problem. Hundreds of girls were huddled on one side of the vast hall, and hundreds of boys were huddled on the other. To get them into eight straight lines, properly paired, took the best part of an hour. Nor was it done without heartache. Some of the girls, poor things, had no partners, and they looked, I fear, as though they never would have. However, a squad or two of officer cadets from the military academy at Wiener Neustadt had been drafted in for the occasion. They performed their duty, but not with grace.

How the professor berated them. He wanted the polonaise done well; he insisted on repeats, and yet more repeats, and yet more. They would be wearing *frack*, would they not? No sloppy turn-out for him. About waltzing, he was positively autocratic. Everybody must do the *Linkswalz*, the *valse renversée*—leading with the right foot instead of the left. The movement is certainly more even, with less pumping up and down of the extended hand. The professor had the authority of Moses upon the mountain. The rows of white faces stared politely. Hundreds of legs obeyed. The one young man who simply would not, could not, lead with the right leg, was singled out. Space was cleared for him. He and his girl had to do it alone, before the hundreds of staring white faces.

Meanwhile, in a side box, the president of the Chemists and Druggists Association was discreetly discussing with a band leader what music would be played and how much it would cost. For 13 orchestral sequences, eight players, eight suppers, the price would be 30,000 schillings. For 17 sequences, nine players, buffet for nine, the bill would be 32,000 schillings (approximately $2,000). This discussion lasted, with intermittent distractions, right through the rehearsal. The tricky business of travelling expenses was mentioned. And the even trickier business of receipts. At last, arrangements were satisfactory. Hands were shaken. The chemists' president then turned to me and warmly invited me to the ball itself a few days

A crowd of young Viennese dance, drink, or simply chat with friends at a street festival in the Naschmarkt in south Vienna. In summer, a round of outdoor neighbourhood parties and fêtes provides freewheeling pop counterparts to the formal balls of the eight-week-winter carnival season known as Fasching.

later. I explained that I had no *frack*, not even a dinner jacket. But allowances were made for this eccentricity: at home, I was made to feel, I no doubt wore *frack* twice a week.

On the evening of the ball I arrived at the palace early. "You know, this is a very important occasion for Vienna," said the serious young usher who showed me to a wonderful place in the best box in a balcony at one end of the sumptuous hall, with a view right down it. I believed him. Professor Fränzl was in resplendent *frack*. The chemists and druggists wore opera cloaks and top hats, known as *Zylinder*, or cylinder hats. Some of them affected pince-nez and monocles. I spotted several senior army officers, proud fathers, their chests a-glitter with medals. Round many a neck hung an enamel cross on a ribbon. To many a lapel was pinned a row of orders. Franz Josef could not have asked for more.

Flowers everywhere. Servants in livery, proper flunkies. By way of an overture, a star from the Volksoper sang songs from Kálmán's operetta *Gräfin Mariza*. A ballet with a Hungarian theme followed. At last, the guests of honour entered in procession, the high and mighty among Viennese chemists. A lady cabinet minister was among them to deliver a short address and declare the ball open. To the music of a polonaise by Ziehrer, *the* promenade of promenades began. In came the professor's well-drilled pupils—long white dresses to the ground, long white gloves to the shoulder, bouquets of flowers, hair arrangements, splendid *frack*. The mammoth *Linkswalz* followed, and it was a triumph. The ball was in full swing and would continue until five in the morning. A thousand and more teenagers, and not one of them misbehaving. The great imperial rooms had surely been more abused than that in the past. Of course, the dancers and their proud parents wanted to be taken for grand folk; of course, they saw themselves as the heirs of archdukes; and if it was *portierisch*—to use the cutting Viennese expression for servants playing at being master—it was also touching. Only the innocent at heart take their pleasures like this.

Music and ceremony go together in Vienna. Even the most solemn music, sung Mass on a Sunday, has an air of entertainment about it. To attend Mass at 9 o'clock in the morning in the Hofburg Chapel—a showpiece occasion—means wearing one's Sunday finest. Tickets for the occasion have to be bought in advance from theatre agencies. A cocktail atmosphere reigns. Sweeping stone stairs lead up to a suite of reception rooms with parquet flooring, and on into what can be described as a series of salons, but are in fact the former imperial boxes, with a view down to the body of the church from the level of the clerestory. The walls of the boxes are covered in magenta silk with a darker floral pattern on it, just like the walls in the private apartments of the Hofburg.

The élite in the boxes, not courtiers any more, but the possessors of higher-priced tickets, are separated from the worshippers in the chapel by glass screens—wonderful screens with mahogany frames and hand-moulded brass hinges; nowadays the élite can have a better view of the service below on closed-circuit television. The Mass is by Mozart, Schubert, Haydn or Bruckner, but the whole performance, with its hint of floor-show, might have come straight from Strauss.

In winter, between October and March, it is customary after Sunday Mass to gravitate to the outdoor skating rink. This has been in existence a mere century or more. Half the site was sold off in the 1960s for development and now contains an American-owned hotel which glowers over the Heumarkt; but what is left is enough for several hundred skaters at a time, and also a small restaurant and changing rooms. Strauss waltzes resound on tinny loudspeakers. This is a club, but anyone can enter by paying at the gate. Members have the advantage of a personal locker and an attendant who will clean their skates.

In the centre of the rink, out of the way of people entering or leaving the ice, two skating circles are roped off for dancing. One is for experts, the other for those who are either aspiring or else too old to be more than stately. The skating standard in both circles is high. Everyone knows the two basic waltz steps on ice: the one inexplicably known as *Java*, in which the couples dance side by side; the other as *Herzlwalz*, or heart-waltz, a reference to the pattern cut by the sudden reverse in the movement. When the music switches into a jolly march, by Strauss usually, the experts from the No. 1 circle whizz away to a roped-off enclave in a corner of the rink for a *Kettenkilian*, an intricate chain-step performed by groups of six, or even eight people, their arms linked round one another's waists. As the chain gathers pace to the music and then has to turn within the area provided, the outside person is whipped around at impressive speed. Properly done, it is thrilling.

Meanwhile the skaters in the No. 2 circle are dancing at a much more sedate pace, the equivalent of doing the breast-stroke in a swimming pool. Cashmere and pearls nestle under fur coats or the green *loden* overcoats and jackets which have been upgraded from traditional peasant costume to be worn by the *Herrschaften*—to use that handy expression covering all the nuances of "ladies and gentlemen". I have seen smart young Viennese men skating around carrying rolled umbrellas just in case it begins to snow, and even a girl with a toy poodle under her arm. Round and round they swirl, as at a cocktail party, forming and re-forming into groups of friends and acquaintances, but always moving anti-clockwise. There is a short break at mid-morning when a machine like a baby bull-dozer is driven over the ice to smooth its surface, and soon it will be time for a whopping, exercise-sharpened lunch.

Another traditional Viennese ceremony takes place in the Opera, and it is especially formal on first nights. By custom, a new production opens

A bunch of pine twigs—the traditional emblem of the Heurigen—indicates that this establishment is open.

A Rustic Tradition

Few places are more quintessentially Viennese than the rustic wine-shops, known as *Heurigen*, which are found principally in the semi-rural suburbs bordering the Wienerwald. The word literally means "this year's" and it refers to the house speciality: wine of the latest vintage sold by the wine-grower himself in the kitchen or garden of his home.

Today many *Heurigen* have become flourishing tourist businesses and older customers grumble at their commercialism. Yet the best of the inns still retain a regular clientele who go to them to taste the sharp young wine, to eat food they have brought with them, and to sing favourite songs accompanied by violin, accordion or zither.

A waitress brings fresh wine to Heurigen customers. Following custom, she will mark up the amount they drink on a piece of paper kept in a glass on their table.

A zitherist entertains customers with songs of Old Vienna at a tavern in the suburb of Salmannsdorf.

on a Sunday, and the first performance is something of an occasion even for those who do not attend. Tension has been building up in the preceding week, with newspaper articles and interviews with the singers. Tickets go on sale on the Tuesday before the opening; many are allocated to the holders of permanent subscriptions, who receive them by mail if they have accounts or else go along to collect them at the advance booking office and simply pay the price as marked on the ticket. Meanwhile, such unallocated tickets as remain are given out to theatre agencies, which mark them up as they see fit.

There is a thriving trade in unwanted subscription tickets. Twenty years ago I used to cultivate a Frau Papp, a lady with the strangest of hair-styles, comprising both braids and a bun, who made a living from the resale of subscription tickets. A one-woman band, she could conjure tickets out of nowhere. I would sit making polite conversation with her, sipping coffee in her room, waiting for her suppliers to arrive; these were not at all black market touts as popularly imagined, but respectable men in horn-rimmed spectacles, Herr Doctors and Herr Hofrats, making a nice profit from their unwanted seats. A similar system, all very furtive and all very expensive, still goes on nowadays.

From Tuesday on, the black-market price climbs day by day, doubling, even trebling. No matter how important the first night is, the *concierges* of Sacher's or the Imperial can always provide a ticket right up to the moment when the curtain rises, but at a mammoth premium. The chic thing to do—barefaced Viennese snobbery—is to arrive at the Opera at the last possible second, abandon the car in front of Sacher's around the corner, tip the doorman to park it, which he will do while mumbling gratefully, "Only for you, Herr Graf," or something else suitable of the sort—maybe "Excellenz must hurry tonight". A last minute rush up the Opera steps, a flinging of coats into the *garde-robe*, hectic passing of small change and numbered slips, the last warning bell, and then no late admittance. Half-way through comes the interval, and the audience begins to troop through the promenade rooms. Here is Viennese ritual at its highest. In recent years the audience has been growing smarter and smarter. It is unthinkable not to wear a dark suit, or evening dress. All want to look their best, even those who can afford only a *stehplatz*, or standing room. Just one more twist of the imagination, and it is possible to think that the most essential feature of the Opera is to see and be seen.

Facing each other in the main promenade hall are busts of two past directors of the Opera: Mahler on one side and Richard Strauss (no relation to Johann) on the other. Strauss's *Salome* was the last new work performed in the imperial Opera, a month before the Emperor Charles's abdication, and his *Rosenkavalier* and *Ariadne* are always in the Opera repertoire. Mahler was the director from 1897 to 1907, four years before his death, and Strauss from 1919 to 1924 (he died in 1949). They are the great dead with whom we may rub shoulders. Household gods. And yet, as directors, both men were harassed and embittered by their stint at the opera. Both of them resigned.

What disturbed them was the way they were dictated to by the musical bureaucrats, a Viennese breed who have shown great staying power. Music in Vienna has always been closely bound to the state, with varying results. In the old days the musical bureaucrats were members of the court who fancied themselves as experts in music and exercised a powerful influence over appointments to key posts, such as the directorship of the Opera. Once Vienna became capital of the Republic, musical life came under the control of professional civil servants, who kept a close eye on box office receipts and tightened their grip on both the purse strings and the musical appointments system.

The embitterment of Mahler and Strauss repeated an old Viennese theme. Few composers were ever free from the need to lobby for patronage from the establishment, nor could they ever quite predict what their fortunes would be. True artists were too often snubbed by the musical bureaucrats during their lifetime and placed on pedestals of honour after their death. Noticing this tendency, many an observer has said, with varying degrees of scorn, that in order to be a genius in Vienna, it is better to be dead. The music critic Heinrich Kralik has explained what lies behind this judgment: "One of the oldest and most deeply seated Viennese characteristics is to cold-shoulder and treat with scepticism verging on personal injury anyone abnormally gifted who happens to be regarded with esteem and admiration by the world at large." The question arises, why did Mozart and Beethoven and the other great names of classical music put up with the Viennese? What was it that kept them in Vienna?

Towards the end of the 18th Century, at least, Vienna was a natural place for a musician to live. First and foremost, there was a ready supply of patronage. The Habsburgs liked and encouraged music. Maria Theresa could sing a soprano part at sight. Her husband, the Emperor Franz played the violin. Schönbrunn and the Hofburg regularly had musical evenings. The musical spirit ran right through the imperial court. Several leading princely families supported their own orchestras and retained composers. Aristocrats like Razumovsky, Waldstein, Liechtenstein, Kinsky, Lichnowsky have been immortalized as patrons and sponsors of Mozart symphonies, Beethoven concertos and other famous works which were dedicated to them in genuine gratitude.

If patronage was Vienna's first attraction, good company was its second. Musicians could live among musicians, tutor each other, attend each other's concerts. One *Kapellmeister*, or musical director, wrote about an opera of his presented in the Lobkowitz Palace (where Beethoven gave

the first performance of his Third Symphony, the "Eroica"): "All the archdukes, the members of high nobility, and the best connoisseurs and dilettanti from Vienna were present. I had the pleasure to see among my listeners Salieri [Mozart's deadly enemy, once supposed to have poisoned him], Beethoven, Weigl, Clementi, Kozeluh, Girowetz, Umlauf and almost everybody else among the *Kapellemeister* and composers who just happen to be here."

Until well into the 19th Century, composers continued to come to Vienna. Indeed, of the many who worked in Vienna in the 18th and 19th Centuries, only two, Franz Schubert and Johann Strauss, were natives of the city. Haydn, perhaps, can also be included since he was born not far away in Lower Austria (at the village of Rohrau). The others were eager for a musical home. But in spite of the obvious advantages of a city with an active musical life, many of them were disappointed with Vienna, staying to make the best of a bad job, if at all.

Haydn was one who was happy with Vienna. He was in general fortunate in his lot as resident composer to the Esterházys, richest of Hungarian princes. One of the most attractive things about him was his generous recognition of his peers. He told Mozart's father that Wolfgang Amadeus was "the greatest composer known to me either in person or by name". Of his one-time pupil Beethoven, he wrote that he "will one day be considered one of Europe's greatest composers and I shall be proud to be called his teacher".

Mozart, the boy prodigy from Salzburg, first came to Vienna with his father to give a concert. A contemporary portrait of him as an eight-year-old at the keyboard—his powdered wig deliciously white, his coat a nursery blue—captures one of those moments of innocent joy as rare as they are powerful. No wonder Maria Theresa hugged him and her daughter Marie Antoinette picked him up and sat him on her lap when

Tributes to the Titans

Although Vienna historically showed scant respect for many great composers while they lived and worked there, the city has been more than generous in bestowing posthumous tributes—particularly in the form of monuments to adorn parks and squares. In the five examples here, described from left to right, now-famous musicians sit in state, surrounded by sculptured muses or admirers.

At the far left, a youthful Wolfgang Amadeus Mozart rises above a swirl of cherubs in the Burggarten—a belated homage unveiled in 1896 by the city that had given him an unmarked grave a century earlier. Franz Schubert sits with scorebook on lap in the Stadtpark. His contemporary, Ludwig van Beethoven, looms with leonine intensity on the Beethovenplatz. In the Resselpark, an effigy of Johannes Brahms listens pensively to a muse of music. And in the Stadtpark, Anton Bruckner modestly averts his gaze from a muse transported with adoration.

he fell over in a corridor. Mozart declared he was going to marry her when he grew up. He touched every heart. Count von Zinzendorf wrote in his diary in 1762: "The poor little chap plays splendidly. He's a witty, quick and charming child."

The nobility condescended to him, and Mozart knew it. Among his many virtues was fortitude; and as an adult, he had to cultivate it in Vienna when he came to stay there periodically with his wife Constanze. To his sister he gave this description of his life in Vienna: "My hair is dressed at six o'clock in the morning, and by seven I am always fully dressed. I then write till nine, and from nine to one give lessons. I then dine, unless I am invited to some house where they dine at two, or even at three o'clock, as, for instance, yesterday and today at the Countess Zichy's and the Countess Thun's. I cannot work before five or six o'clock in the evening, and even then I am often prevented by a concert. If not, I write till nine o'clock. I then go to see my dear Constanze."

Among the great works he wrote in Vienna were *Figaro* and the "Jupiter" symphony. But the longer he lived there, the less he liked it. His success faltered. The Viennese did not appreciate his music. He was commissioned only intermittently to write new works and his patrons did not pay promptly. Among the best of them was the Emperor Josef II himself, but Mozart felt used and patronized by him. In 1782, at the age of 26, he was writing contemptuously: "These Viennese gentry (by which I chiefly mean the Emperor) must not imagine that I am in the world purely for the sake of Vienna!" Five years later he accepted the job of chamber-music composer from the Emperor, but after Josef's death in 1790, he ran into severe financial difficulties and ill-health. He was soon on his deathbed, weeping for what he had not had time to compose. His Requiem lay unfinished on his table, and he was destitute. He was 35 when he was buried in an unmarked grave. The pathos of Mozart's fate goes a long way towards destroying Vienna's reputation as a city where musical genius is specially cherished.

Beethoven lived there for much of his adult life, drawn by his patrons and the company of other musicians. The best thing he found to say about Vienna was that bits of landscape, like near-by Herzogenburg, reminded him of his own Rhineland. Beethoven had awkward habits, such as playing the piano at two in the morning and throwing a bucket of cold water over himself in the middle of his room when he felt hot. He grumbled in his letters about the iniquity of landlords and housekeepers who obliged him to be constantly changing his lodgings. To him, landlords were either extortionate or noisy. Even without his deafness, he was withdrawing into himself. On the other hand he was better at arranging his financial affairs than Mozart and knew how to look after himself. The Viennese always deferred to him, but treated him as an uncomfortable stranger in their midst. Nobody seems to have protested when, at the beginning of this century, the house where Beethoven wrote some of his last works and where he died in 1827, was pulled down.

Public neglect was Schubert's lot in his home city. He was too modest to struggle for fame; he was content to live in a charmed circle of professional musicians and painters. He was a member of the Society of Friends of Music; his C Major Symphony, known as the Great, was commissioned, but then rejected by this body in 1828 on the grounds that it was too long and too difficult to play. Twenty years were to pass before Mendelssohn took it up and conducted it at Leipzig, to general applause. Indeed, not until his premature death at the age of 31 was Schubert recognized for the great composer he was. He left masses of posthumous works, including lost operas and symphonies: somebody someday may find them.

Brahms had drifted to Vienna from Hamburg in 1862, partly out of unhappiness, partly to take a job as conductor of a choral society. It seems that he wanted to leave Germany to avoid being in the same country as Wagner, then the leading German composer, who—with typical crazy venom—called him a "Jewish csárdás player". Three years as director of the society, from 1872 to 1875, were enough. He felt cramped by the musical bureaucrats and resigned. He travelled widely but came back to Vienna, for the sake of its associations with the great composers. It was Brahms perhaps who did more than anyone to romanticize Vienna, saying that it was sacred to him as the world's musical capital.

Mahler's time in Vienna was more stormy than Brahms's. He was never made an honorary member of the Society, as other distinguished composers were, Brahms included. Like so many who have enriched Vienna, he came from a small German-speaking enclave in Bohemia, where his Jewish father ran a small drinks shop. He was a pianist to begin with, a prodigy. By 1886, when he was only 26, he was already launched on a public career as conductor and artistic director of the Budapest Opera.

The composer Arnold Schoenberg (above), 31 years old when he sat for the Austrian artist Richard Gerstl in 1905, was the enfant terrible of 20th-Century Viennese music. Almost entirely self-taught, he abandoned traditional ideas of tone in the quest for a personal musical style, and at least one of his works caused a riot when it was first performed. Schoenberg himself painted a portrait (right) of his pupil in Vienna, Alban Berg, whose application of his master's theories did much to win them both the wide recognition they enjoy today.

There he felt persecuted, partly because of anti-semitism. By 1897 he was in Vienna, as director of the Opera. The city's musical politics, he immediately discovered, were a bugbear—and friends at court were indispensable. A series of petty rows came to a head when he no longer commanded the support of the palace chamberlain, Prince Montenuovo, and Mahler's resignation followed.

Arnold Schoenberg came up against the same prejudices at the turn of the century, although his modernism also offended tradition. He and Alban Berg and Anton von Webern, the last composers of note to have come out of Vienna, were subjected to attacks that Mozart and Schubert at least were spared. The audience for Schoenberg consisted of a handful prepared to be open-minded about avant-garde music. Musicians alone were receptive to his *Verklärte Nacht*, composed in Vienna in 1899. About his life in Vienna before the First World War, Schoenberg was later to write, "I had had to fight for every new work; I had been offended in the most outrageous manner by criticism; I had lost friends. And I stood alone in a world of enemies." He ended his days in 1951 as an emigré in America.

Most of these men, certainly Mahler and Schoenberg, would have been unhappy anywhere. It was not entirely Vienna's fault that they failed to fit in. Anton Bruckner, for example, organist in the Hofburg Chapel in Franz Josef's heyday, did his work year in and year out, wrote his symphonies, and died a fulfilled man. But as the 19th Century drew to an end, composers generally received less esteem, and there was less and less patronage to be had in the city. Brahms was the last innovative composer for whom Viennese society put itself out.

It is ironic that, at a moment when no more Mahlers or Brahmses appear in sight, the state does more than ever to encourage or attract musical talent, at least financially. The same goes for literature—the government's annual subsidy for music and theatre combined has been calculated at four million schillings a day, give or take some percentage points for inflation. Without support of this magnitude, the performing arts and music would be in distress in Vienna, a sad fact which applies, of course, to all capitals. What stultifies Viennese musical life is not the lack of goodwill or money, but the insistence on accepted forms by bureaucracy and audiences alike. Music in Vienna has become more a matter of ritual than of genuine appreciation. In the concert programmes there is little straying from the familiar Haydn-Mozart-Schubert-Beethoven-Brahms grooves; there is almost no experiment, and practically a ban on novelty. The public will pay only for what they know and enjoy and they will damn a performer or conductor who varies any tempo or reading which over the years has come to be accepted.

I remember once hearing Karl Böhm, the first director of the rebuilt Opera after the last war, conduct the opera *Valkyrie* at an unusual tempo.

The audience disapproved so strongly that they hissed until he changed it in mid-performance. Böhm had the advantage of being Viennese, but the newspapers were full of leaked stories about how his style or his management failed to please the bureaucrats with the purse strings. In 1955, only one year after taking up the appointment, he resigned. Other conductors at the Opera, Herbert von Karajan and Leonard Bernstein for example, have been involved in spectacular rows.

Another sign of contracting musical horizons is the sad decline of amateur playing. In Vienna there have always been cultivated groups of amateurs and music-lovers who studied scores or played instruments for the delight of it. Doctors in particular have had this reputation, ever since the days when Dr. Theodor Billroth, the famous surgeon, invited Brahms to give concerts at his house. Such men of all-round excellence have dwindled to a hard core. Some say that before the Second World War there were more than a thousand private string quartets in Vienna, some say there were only 150. Some say that nowadays there are 70, some say there are only four. I know that only twice in my life have I heard amateurs arranging to make music together in Vienna.

Perhaps 800 professional musicians make a living in the city and a good many of them do keep up the tradition of forming private chamber orchestras or quartets among themselves. But mostly they are busy fulfilling their official duties. Approximately 150 of the professionals are members of the Vienna Philharmonic Orchestra, eminent in the world since its foundation in 1842. Its members are paid employees of the state and have a contract to play as required at the Opera. That engagement lasts all the year round except for a summer break. In addition, the orchestra gives regular subscription concerts. The profits from these are shared out among the players, on top of their salaries. As at the Opera, any subscription ticket holder automatically gets a seat at each of the scheduled concerts. Since subscription concerts were introduced by the orchestra in 1860 and subscription holders have been increasing in numbers ever since, it is now virtually impossible for anyone without a subscription to attend a Vienna Philharmonic concert. Indeed, in order for all the ticket holders to attend, each cycle of concerts has to be repeated.

Since 1870, the orchestra has had a permanent home at the Musikverein, just off the Ring. The building is just as Brahms saw it, a great pile in confident red brick, with a marble and porphyry interior and the requisite gilding and plaster, worthy of the great institutions of state farther down the Ring. The concert hall has superb acoustics as well.

I visited it one afternoon to see Professor Hübner, the first violinist and, at that time, chairman of the 12-man committee chosen from among the players to deal with the daily running of the orchestra. He had the air of a kindly intellectual, with a habit of pushing his spectacles off his nose and on to his forehead. He explained that the members of the

Members of the Austrian Pensioners' Association who have formed a mandolin orchestra assemble on a fire escape outside the building where they rehearse. The pensioners are affiliated to the Austrian Socialist Party and often perform at political functions.

orchestra play in string quartets, an octet, a quintet, a wind quintet, a wind ensemble and a chamber ensemble as well as perform with the full orchestra. "We nearly all teach in the high schools or the Conservatoire, the college of music," said Professor Hübner. "It is the best way of knowing what talent is coming up.

"Yes, I regret it is impossible to get tickets for our subscription concerts. The 4,000 subscription holders more than fill the hall. Some of those subscription holders have had their seats for at least 50 years and relinquish them only on death. Luckily the right to seats can't be inherited or there'd be no movement at all."

If traditionalism is the most Viennese of virtues, then the Vienna Boys Choir is the most Viennese of musical institutions. It is a charming period piece that has been brilliantly streamlined to cope with the present. Unlike the Vienna Philharmonic, it has managed to survive without state subsidy. Its continuity in the face of adversity endears it to the public, which finds comfort where it can, especially in something so close to real-life operetta as the Boys Choir.

The Emperor Maximilian founded the boys choir in 1498, to sing in the Hofburg. Schubert belonged to the choir from 1808 to 1813. Christoph Willibald von Gluck, the court composer in the mid-18th Century, wrote music for the boys. As organist in the Hofburg after 1867, Bruckner worked with them every week. The downfall of the Habsburgs in 1918 left the choir without a patron and without a role. To reform as a private institution, once the old society had become unstuck, was a gesture pregnant with nostalgia for the past and hope for the future.

Josef Schnitt, ex-chaplain at the Hofburg, raised funds for the boys between 1918 and 1924, founded the Choir Boys Institute to house and school them, and put them back on a stable footing. The old court uniform the boys had worn, similar to that of a page or a cadet, was clearly out of place in the new era. Instead Director Schnitt chose to dress the choir in sailor suits, because that was how properly brought-up little boys had appeared on Sundays before the First World War. That was a touch of genius. Every Austrian automatically feels parental interest in the well-scrubbed, bright-eyed boys who embellish and enliven Christmas and Easter, ceremonies religious as well as civic, who sing anthems and light Viennese songs, and carols such as *Silent Night* with the perfect purity of tone that comes from hard training.

From 1924 to 1945, the choir had no home base, but Director Schnitt put that straight when, in 1948, he leased the Augarten Palace from the government. This beautiful Baroque building, dating from the 17th Century, adjoins the famous Augarten porcelain factory in the Leopoldstadt, Vienna's 2nd District to the east of the Danube Canal. The Emperor Joseph II spent summer seasons in it, and the last Emperor Charles was brought up there. Successive chancellors of the Republic once used the palace as an official residence. Director Schnitt had to borrow money to repair war damage and provide furnishings.

The second director of the choir is Walter Tautschnig, an ex-choir boy himself, who took over from Schnitt in 1955. During his tenure he has added a modern wing complete with swimming pool and gymnasium. Dr. Tautschnig is energetic, in good trim, obviously immersed in the job. "We have four choirs altogether," he says, "two of them always on tour, and one always on duty here. The tours are the highlight of a boy's time, and provide us with a large part of our income. We've had dozens of tours to America, several to Asia and Australia. It's the bait, so to speak. It's why we have candidates enough for our auditions, which are twice a year, in February and September."

The school is spotlessly clean, the dormitories tidy as barrack-rooms, the new wing airy and spacious. It might be a rather tough English boarding school. Discipline sits in the air. The director believes in football to release energies, in snowball fights in winter, and in walking tours in the mountains, where the boys spend their summer holidays. *Mens sana in corpore sano.* Those boys who are accepted for the choir must make the best of their short careers. A treble voice in a boy breaks at about 12, and then he must hand in his sailor suit.

Excellence is what the Vienna Boys Choir is about—excellence, perfectionism, in an egalitarian city where such virtues are hard to come by. Director Tautschnig knows that he is moving against the grain of the times: "Mothers no longer sing to their children as they used to. Our musicality is vanishing, what with the radio and television. Every year it's harder to keep up standards of excellence in a world which doesn't care for it." No doubt about it, the boys are able to take advantage of privileges; they are in a position to experience star quality before their contemporaries have understood that there is such a thing.

The director takes me out into the park, over to the preparatory school where the smaller boys are having lessons. They stand up when we enter, they chorus, *"Grüss Gott"*. Soon it is time for break and one of them, a freckled child with carroty hair, rushes up to the director and clings to him. "Homesick?" the director asks. The boy nods, and says what Mozart had also said in his childhood letters home, "It's hard to leave your mother when you're only eight".

A Unique and Pure-toned Instrument

At a concert in the Augarten Palace, sailor-suited choirboys show equal precision in performing some light classical songs and in acknowledging applause.

One of the sturdiest pillars of Vienna's reputation as a musical capital is the Vienna Boys Choir. Throughout the world, the 88 boy singers who make up the four performing choirs are known and admired for their professional approach and purity of tone. The Choir occupies suitably grand premises in the Augarten Palace, a former imperial hunting lodge that has been converted into a boarding school. Choirboys spend seven months of each year there, receiving an academic education as well as music lessons from a teaching staff of 30. The rest of their time (apart from three months' holiday) is given over to international tours, whose proceeds finance the running of the school. A chorister's association with the Choir need not end when his voice breaks: he can continue to live at the palace, even if he finishes his education elsewhere.

In a dormitory in the palace, some of the choirboys fold their bedspreads before starting their daily school programme: four and a half hours of lessons and two hours' homework, plus two hours of choir rehearsals.

A youngster leaps to head the ball during an impromptu soccer match in the palace grounds. During the three hours set aside each day for recreation, pupils can also use the swimming-pool, or play badminton or handball.

A teacher conducts a lesson from a piano cluttered with music and a bust of an old choirboy: Franz Schubert.

Towards Note-perfect Performances

A rigorous musical discipline underlies the Choir's excellence. Children wishing to join the Choir start taking voice lessons at the age of eight, at a preparatory school in the Augarten Palace park. Those who meet the expected standards are enrolled in the Choir two years later. Even though the average performing life lasts less than four years, the training is rarely wasted; many of the boys go on to careers as professional musicians.

Framed by a window sash, a rehearsing choirboy concentrates intently on a score. All the boys are able to sight-read as a matter of course.

In the grounds of the Augarten Palace, uniformed choirboys stroll through a formal garden decorated with topiary and a 12-foot-high ornamental urn.

Facing an altarpiece painted in 1730 by the Italian artist Martino Altomonte, the Choir's director leads the boys through a concert given in the chapel of St. Bernard in the Inner City. The Choir's annual visit to the chapel to celebrate the start of the Vienna Festival—a six-week programme of music and drama held in the late spring—is one of the more picturesque events in a calendar of engagements that averages 400 performances a year.

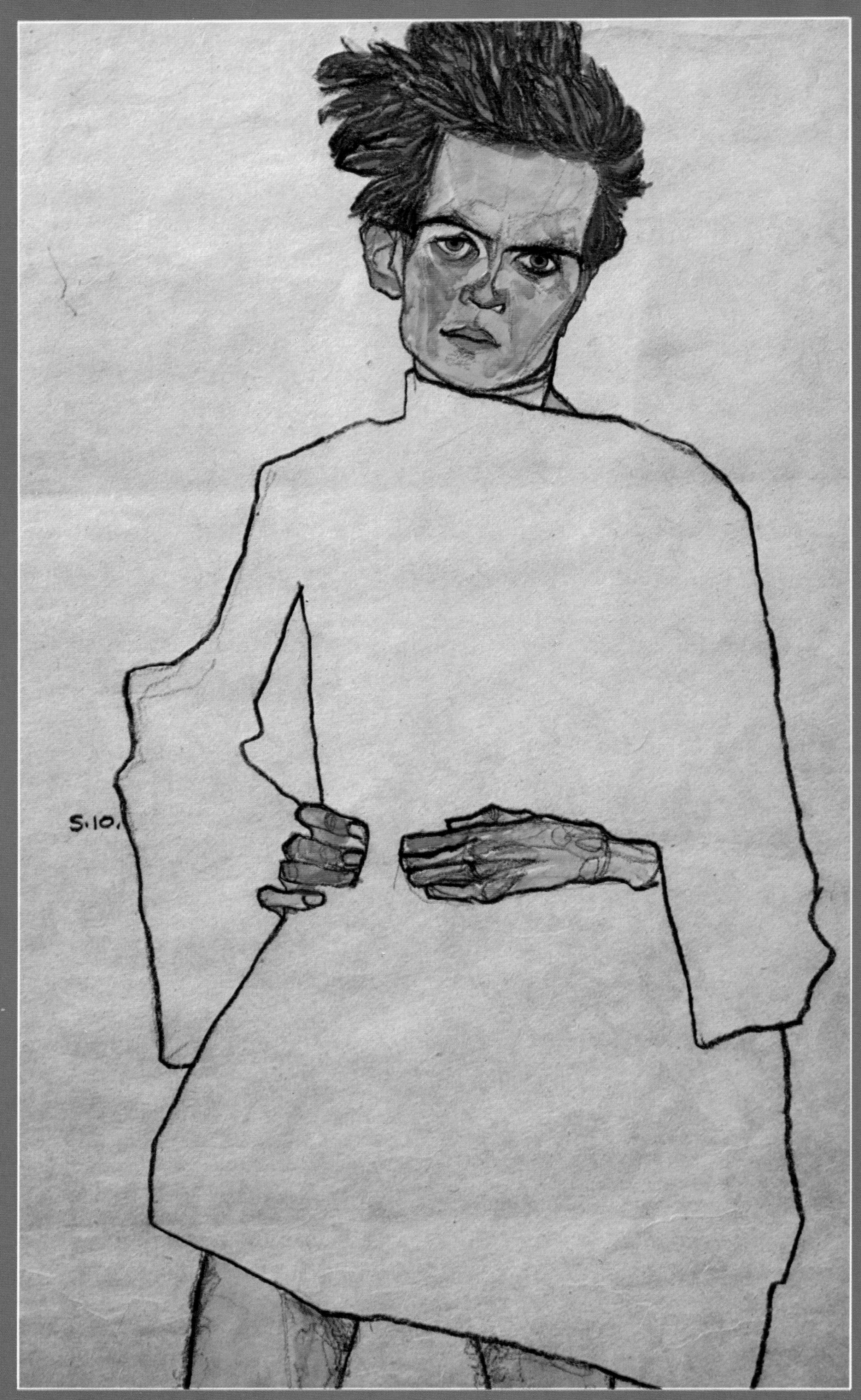
S.10.

6

The Gay Apocalypse

If ever there was a time when it was bliss to be alive in Vienna, it was during the 20 or 30 years before the First World War. But it was the bliss of sunset, not of dawn. People in the capital felt they had to enjoy themselves while there was still the chance to do so. Outwardly, the show was worthy of a great European capital. Heads of state, from King Edward VII to Kaiser Wilhelm and the Russian Grand-dukes, passed through the city: they disported themselves at vast ceremonial banquets and troop reviews, then spent a month sipping restorative mineral waters at Marienbad or Karlsbad. Inwardly, a sense of unease prevailed. The monarchs and their courtiers and the frock-coated newspaper correspondents following in their train noted that Austro-Hungarian parliaments in Budapest and Vienna were being called and dissolved rather rapidly—too rapidly, really—for an autocratic empire. Such topics as "Vienna and the Balkans" or "The Nationalities Problem" agitated diplomats and columnists.

Meanwhile, the Emperor Franz Josef continued as robust as ever, up at six in the morning for the state papers, lunching off his favourite boiled beef with horseradish sauce, and in bed by nine at night whenever possible. The basic unit of the Austrian currency—the crown—was a gold piece as solid and reassuring as the Emperor himself. The newly completed grand buildings along the Ringstrasse were resplendent, the theatres and concert halls played to full houses, and society appeared to be harmoniously united. In the Prater, the park and former game reserve where the imperial family and the aristocracy still paraded in their carriages or on horseback, the poor and unemployed of the city came to gawp at the great and wealthy, but not yet to shake their fists. The giant Ferris wheel was put up in the Prater in 1898 as a symbol of Austrian progressiveness, a riposte to the Eiffel Tower, built nine years earlier. It was also an offering of bread and circuses to the Austrian public, a gesture in the direction of social peace. In both roles it stood as a monument to the delusions of the age.

If the underlying facts of life were ugly, there was no need to confront them too directly. That was the feeling of the old regime. Enjoy what was enjoyable, ignore everything else. When a fashionable theatre burned down in 1881, with the loss of 400 lives, the chief of the fire brigade reported to the Emperor's uncle, the Archduke Albrecht, who was sent down to inspect the scene of the disaster: "Everybody was saved." Why upset the Emperor, poor old man? Why should anyone be upset? No Golden Age would be complete without its self-deception. Hermann

A half sorrowing, half sinister self-portrait by the Viennese artist Egon Schiele foreshadows his own early death in 1918 at the age of 28. Obsessed with sex, decay and retribution, his paintings express the desperate hedonism of Vienna in the last days of the empire.

A watercolour by Rudolf von Alt catalogues the sumptuous art works in the studio of Hans Makart, a successful Viennese painter of the mid-19th Century.

Broch, the Viennese novelist who revelled in stylish contradictions, coined the phrase "Gay Apocalypse" for the whole period.

The phrase neatly captured the tensions of this society at its close. The end of a great empire can be as full of interest and excitement as its heyday, and in Vienna around the turn of the century, uncertainty and instability led to final bursts of glory. As the political strength of the Habsburg Empire ebbed, the creative energies of the capital expressed themselves in the arts and sciences. In their feverish experimentalism, writers, architects and artists appeared to be engaged in a battle of life and death. Some were prophets farsighted enough to predict the approaching end, and perhaps they even hoped to stave it off. Others were doom-sayers or scathing satirists or clowns, enmeshed in the process of decay and unable to see their way to personal escape.

When the empire collapsed—as everyone, deep down, had known it would—the talent in Vienna began to drift away. Without political strength to sustain it, the old cultural life fell apart with ever-increasing speed, and when Hitler arrived in 1938, it entered its final death throes. The drift of talent became a rush to escape, and the stage was cleared for Nazi society. And yet, even after the end had come, not everyone could accept it. The fall-out from the explosion continues to this very day.

Looking back over the lives of those creative spirits who rose to prominence during the Gay Apocalypse, and seeing what happened to them in the aftermath, one can watch the long drawn-out process of disintegration taking place. The first step in that process was a declaration of no confidence in the past. The departure came in the arts, which seemed to benefit most noticeably from the contradictions of the times.

Early in 1898, a structure as striking as the giant Prater wheel, but utterly different in conception, was built in Vienna: an exhibition hall on the Naschmarkt nicknamed the Mahdi's Tomb (an echo from the Sudan, where General Gordon, hero of Victorian England, and a Dervish rebel named the Mahdi were in the news). It was given this name because of its chunky, orientalized façade and its globule of a dome, with a lacework of gilded cast-iron all over it. The hall was a monument to change. Its architect, Josef Olbrich, was one of the foremost artists of the Secessionist Movement, named to describe its members' break-away from Austria's conservative Art Institute. The movement aimed to pursue a new idiom appropriate to youth, the *Jugendstil* or art nouveau whose free-flowing curves and gentle motifs drawn from nature had begun to influence architecture and interior decoration in Europe in the 1880s; it stood for the future which was fermenting in the decay of the past. Besides Olbrich, the main Secessionist artists and designers were Gustav Klimt, Otto Wagner, and also Josef Hoffman, an arts-and-crafts man who went on to found a famous workshop, the Wiener Werkstätte.

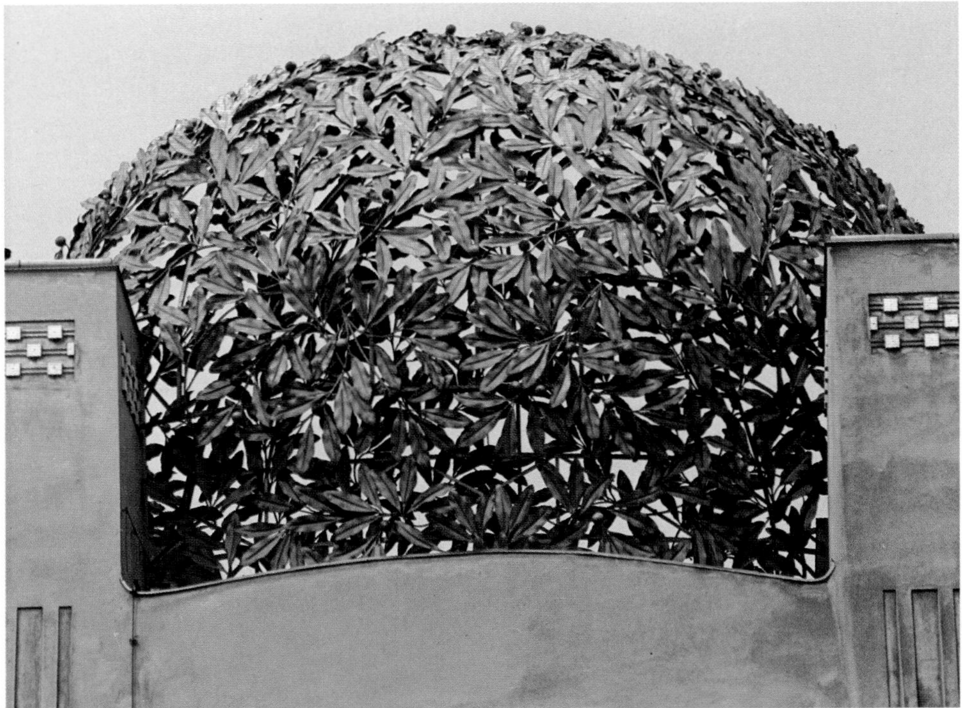

A lattice of 3,000 cast-iron leaves serves as a cupola for the Secession Building, home of Vienna's anti-establishment artists at the turn of the century. The spectacularly domed exhibition hall designed by the influential Secessionist architect Josef Olbrich in 1898, soon acquired a variety of local nicknames such as "the golden cabbage".

The Secessionists and their pupils held regular exhibitions in their eye-catching new hall until the outbreak of the First World War, when their belief in beauty, truth and goodness was sadly overtaken by events. The whole movement fell to pieces, but many of their works survive. Here and there across Vienna are frond-like *Jugendstil* lines or outlines: a roof silhouette, balconies, tidbits of decor or interior design, and the whole splendiferous French embassy with peppermint-green decorations, located on the Schwarzenbergplatz.

The most notable monument to the epoch is the Stadtbahn, or city railroad, which supplements the tramway system and runs along the outer ring-road, or Gürtel. Otto Wagner had won the commission to design it in 1894. He was a professor in the Academy of Arts and turned a piece of fine engineering into public art. The Stadtbahn is elevated on arches, and therefore well exposed to view. Its stations are stately whitened temples, elegantly Hellenistic, with a hint of Mesopotamia about them. A few of these stations, at the more important stops, are art nouveau follies—wonderful conceits in cast-iron, their loops and struts brilliantly blending invention and workmanship.

Otto Wagner continually explored new forms. The Kirche am Steinhof, a large-domed church built between 1905 and 1907, earned him a reputation as an inspired adaptor of classical themes; the building is all clean lines and clean taste. At the same moment he was sobering down to functional ideas. His large Postsparkassenamt, the Post Office Savings Bank, is upright and chunky and looks ahead to the mainstream of the 20th Century. Wagner was accustoming himself to such utilitarian things as efficient use of space.

At the beginning of the century, the Secessionists were overtaken on the road to modernism by people more extreme and experimental, whose ideas foreshadowed the grimmer aspects of the future. Among them was Adolf Loos. In 1893, at the age of 23, he had set off for America, and in Chicago had come under the influence of Louis Sullivan, who pioneered the concept of skyscrapers. On his return to Vienna, Loos was keen to

"The Arts lead us into the Kingdom of the Ideal," claimed the Secessionist Gustav Klimt, who in 1902 painted this portrait of Emilie Flöge, the owner of a fashionable Viennese dress shop. The work, combining photographic realism with abstract patterns, typifies the group's taste for the original and the exotic.

introduce revolutionary techniques of architecture. His chance came in 1910 when he designed a shop for Messrs. Goldman and Salatsch on a corner of the Michaelerplatz. He made good use of an irregular site, but the design was so tidy and functional—especially the windows, which were nothing but casements—that "the house without eyebrows", as it was called, became something of a joke. Part of the laugh was its juxtaposition with the incredibly pompous carriage entrance to the Hofburg on the far side of the square—the gate was a part of the imperial palace that had been finished in the previous decade, although it was centuries older in spirit. Loos liked to tease.

Ornament was a crime in Loos's eyes, and he published aggressive essays to say so. He wanted structures to speak for themselves, their form dictated by their purpose. He worshipped flatness and exposed beams and the shock of unadorned functionalism. This was all very fine in the overblown heyday of *Jugendstil*, when the Bauhaus school in Germany and its "machines for living" and the modern school of architectural brutalism had not yet emerged to transform the world's cities. A plain building here and there by Loos provided novelty and did little damage to the urban environment. But in every cost-calculated, mass-produced block in the world today, there is a vein of Loos's theories. Unwittingly, he helped to make ugliness respectable.

Loos and his first wife Lina belonged to that small, hard-core set of bohemians who could be styled as the pace-setters of the Gay Apocalypse. The leading personalities in the set included the writers Stefan Zweig, Ferenc Molnar, Peter Altenberg, Franz Theodor Csokor, and Egon Friedell; the prominent critic, Hermann Bahr; the actor Alexander Girardi; and Hugo von Hofmannsthal, poet and librettist for Richard Strauss. In their lives and loves, one can hardly help seeing the confusions of the period. A few remarkable women acted as catalysts for their social merry-go-round, and Lina Loos was one of them. She was the daughter of Herr Obertimpfler, owner of one of Vienna's historic coffee-houses, the Casa Piccola. She was 16 when Loos first proposed to her and 20 when she finally accepted him. By then, she possessed a reputation as the most beautiful woman in Vienna. Within a year she left Loos and went on to become a cabaret diseuse and actress. Writers and artists gathered about her, and later she related their doings in her interesting memoirs. In the meantime, Loos married three more times, and one more of his ex-wives wrote memoirs in which his name was prominent. In all, hundreds of memoirs were written by or about this bohemian set, and they reveal the desperate pace at which names and loves and hates went round and round.

In attracting gifted men, another member of the set, Alma Schindler, outdid Lina Loos. She was the daughter of a society painter who had Habsburg patrons and shared a studio with Hans Makart, once a fashion-

Contrasting posters by Alfred Roller (above) and Koloman Moser (left) advertise turn-of-the-century Secessionist exhibitions, as well as publicizing the group's official organ, "Ver Sacrum"—Sacred Spring. The shows proved so popular that a critic could write, "The whole of Vienna has become Secessionist".

able painter of gigantic canvases for Ringstrasse houses. Her mother later married Carl Moll, a Secessionist painter. Through Carl Moll, Alma met Gustav Klimt while still an unformed teenager, and he had kissed her. It was her first grand passion, although it never came to anything.

Her first marriage was to Gustav Mahler. She and Mahler were both guests, in the autumn of 1901, at a party given in the house of Berta Zuckerkandl—wife of a famous anatomist, sister-in-law of the French statesman Clemenceau, and author of precisely the memoirs to be expected from someone whose name means Sugar-stick. Mahler was twice Alma's age, but after the party he sent her an unsigned poem. Fifty years later, in *And the Bridge is Love*, her own sugar-stick recollections, Alma wrote: "Mahler, the ascetic, had the reputation of a rake, a corrupter of all the young females in his ensemble. Actually, he was a child and afraid of women. It took me, a silly, inexperienced girl, to bring down his guard." By March, 1902, after Mahler's Fourth Symphony had had its première, they were married in the Karlskirche.

Mahler's music is pure *Jugendstil* in its romanticism and its sensuality, even when a little foetid; but he touched on deeper aspirations. How could such a true genius have virtually eloped with an egregious nymphet? She led him a song and dance until his premature death in 1911. She led everyone a song and dance, including her next husbands, the German-American architect and Bauhaus-founder Walter Gropius and the writer Franz Werfel, author of *The Song of Bernadette.* Long after the Second World War, Alma was still to be seen in the front row of boxes in theatres and operas in New York or European capitals, got up like the prow of a ship, unsinkable, with the same survivor's instinct that kept so many women of the Gay Apocalypse afloat long after their husbands and lovers had lost the struggle against penury and exile and death.

In the light of the abrupt end that Nazism put to their world, the lives of those bohemian pace-setters appear rather dismal. What looked bright then is seen to have been doomed. At best, oblivion awaited them; at worst, emigration or suicide. The writers, even Molnar and Zweig, great as they were considered to be, now seem to blur into one another at the edges. All had similar experiences within a small world which was far more imitative and parochial than was realized at the time.

There was one forecaster at work during the Gay Apocalypse who was accurate enough to gain a lasting reputation: Theodor Herzl. He came from a Jewish family in Budapest. He had always wanted to write, and in 1887, at the age of 27, he appeared in print for the first time in the pages of the *Neue Freie Presse.* This great newspaper had been founded in 1864. Monarchist, legitimist, tradition-minded but not intolerant, it set public opinion. Its editors were great men in the land. Its speciality was the *feuilleton*, an essay or set-piece, midway between reporting and editorializing. Herzl proved expert at this kind of writing.

He had studied law at Vienna University, but did not take it seriously. He was a dandy, unhappy in love, and thought his talent lay in writing for the theatre. But then he found a cause to adopt. As the *Neue Freie Presse* correspondent in Paris, he attended the notorious trial in 1894 of Captain Alfred Dreyfus, the Jewish officer who was falsely accused of treason and imprisoned. Herzl was shattered by this scandal of anti-semitism in action. He could easily see such legal travesties happening in Vienna, whose mayor at that time was Karl Lueger, a well-known anti-semite. Lueger was the man who, when challenged to explain why he had Jewish friends, replied with the notorious remark, "I decide who is a Jew". Herzl had caught the first tremors and warnings of the earthquake to come and now turned himself into the impresario of Zionism.

Herzl's remedy against anti-semitism was to argue in favour of a new homeland for the Jews. In this he was following a policy of nationalism similar to that of other minorities within the Habsburg Empire—the Czechs or South Slavs or Hungarians—who were agitating for independence. About 200,000 Jews lived in Vienna at the time (today there are perhaps 8,000). Most of them, including some editors of the *Neue Freie Presse*, were aghast at Herzl's published proposal that Jews should return to Palestine. By all except a very few, Herzl was ridiculed; he was compared to Jules Verne. But Herzl set about getting his own way in the practical Viennese manner, using his charm and his contacts to lobby

Designed in 1898 by the Secessionist architect Otto Wagner for a house in the Maria-Hilf district, this staircase sets off an art nouveau wrought-iron balustrade against the more functional lines of the walls and windows. Wagner was one of the first architects in Europe to react against heavy ornamentation.

the great and influential. Oddly assorted barons and potentates and adventurers listened to him. The Viennese expression *ante-chambrieren* describes his method in a word: Herzl was a master of the politics of ante-chambers. The first Zionist Congress, staged in Basle in 1897, was his achievement. At the meeting—which made Zionism a political movement—Herzl predicted that within 50 years a Jewish state would be founded. He was almost exactly right; it was founded in May, 1948. Herzl lived long enough to be treated by the Jewish proletariat as a kind of uncrowned king, but he died in 1904, exhausted—aged only 44.

Herzl had felt in his bones that the break-up of the Habsburg Empire would lead to an explosion of German nationalism in which the Jews would have no place. Like Freud, he had the gift of interpreting the signs and portents of his culture; and what he found valid for himself was valid for others. That the Jews tried harder as citizens of the empire but achieved less acceptance than others was not news; but it required astonishing foresight to see where the logic of excluding Jews would lead. Who can say how many hunted people in the end had their lives saved because they were able to escape out of darkness to the tiny utopian patch so strangely blue-printed by an ace *feuilletoniste* of the *Neue Freie Presse*?

One of the most savage critics writing during this period was Karl Kraus, who single-handedly published a journal called *Die Fackel*, meaning "torch" or "fire-brand". From 1899 until 1936, *Die Fackel* appeared irregularly, not quite quarterly, and it perfectly expressed Kraus's tormented personality. When Karl was two, his father, a wealthy Jewish manufacturer, had made the classic move to Vienna from a small town in Bohemia, just as Freud's father had done when Freud was four. But Kraus had curvature of the spine, and never overcame his complex about being a cripple. By temperament he enjoyed tilting against the world, and his ugliness always spurred him on. He appointed himself keeper and treasurer of the German language, which he then proceeded to squander prodigally, obsessively, commenting acidly on everything under the sun.

It was Kraus's delight to cut down rivals mercilessly. He waged war against another newspaper publisher, a Hungarian by the name of Imre Békássy. "*Wien ist verpestet*", Kraus said; "Vienna is pestiferated"—a pun aimed at Békássy's origins in Budapest. He had a running battle with Johannes Schober, the Chief of Police in Vienna, whom he accurately accused of massacring nearly a hundred demonstrators and bystanders during riots at a workers' demonstration in 1927. (Schober later became Chancellor of Austria.) One of Kraus's most biting remarks was at Freud's expense: "Psychoanalysis is that spiritual disease which considers itself its own cure." He savaged the German critic Alfred Kerr, and he savaged the theatre at large, including various producers who might otherwise

The architect Adolf Loos (above) was the leading exponent of functionalism in turn-of-the-century Vienna. In 1910 he designed a corner block for the Michaelerplatz, here framed by the ornate ironwork of a Hofburg Palace gateway. The building, dubbed "the house without eyebrows" because of its unadorned windows, so upset the Emperor Franz Josef that he never used that palace entrance again.

have staged the many plays he wrote. He savaged capitalism and the rich, and the poor, and the Jews, and war, and business, and politics—and finally he drove himself into utter isolation. He was one of those terrible 20th-Century nihilists who have looked on despair and rejoiced, and he reminds one of the German dramatist Bertolt Brecht, and even more of Louis-Ferdinand Céline, the mad French doctor who wrote *Journey to the End of the Night*, a tormented novel in which the fabric of the world seems to become unravelled.

Kraus's dramatic masterpiece, never produced on stage, is appropriately called *The Last Days of Mankind*, and it has a cult-following, although it is hard to stomach because of its enormous length. If staged, it would last at least 10 hours. Staying-power appeared to be his way of overcoming the irredeemable Viennese levity. Yet when Hitler was already casting his shadow over Austria, Kraus fizzled out. He wrote simply, "Nothing occurs to me about Hitler." *Die Fackel* evidently had nothing more to say of any value, nor had Kraus. He had satirized and scourged everything, but by declining to comment on Hitler, he was, by default, encouraging a future which would have no place in it for him. That's what happened in the Gay Apocalypse.

A far gentler satirist, but no less penetrating on the crisis of Vienna, was Robert Musil. His novel, *The Man Without Qualities*, must be one of the longest ever published, more than 2,000 pages in several volumes. Many chapters were written but never printed, and the novel was never completed because Musil could not make up his mind about what he had to say. Like Kraus, he wanted to have a go at everything, but he did at least realize that if you pull the world to pieces, you may have to live among the ruins—and he did not care for that. His man without qualities, Ulrich, was a projection of himself. Musil, born in 1880, had been educated as an engineer and mathematician. He subsequently took a degree in philosophy, writing a thesis on Ernst Mach, the Viennese philosopher around whom a whole group coalesced. Both scientist and artist, Musil could see every side of a question, which was a hindrance to the great actions of which he—and his hero, Ulrich—might have been capable.

Ulrich is Viennese Man. His father supports him. He acquires women easily, and treats them how he pleases. His friends are interesting, his house beautiful, and so much is worth doing that he does very little. Yet he is caught up by pity for a man who committed a senseless murder, and he also involuntarily becomes secretary to a Count Leinsdorf who is running a patriotic, but largely hot-air, campaign to promote the true values of imperial Austria—whatever they may be. Ulrich is liberal, decent, but passive—in the last resort, wasted. He could agree with Kraus's remark that Vienna was "a proving ground of world destruction". Ulrich was all the more refined because his hands had no prospect of getting dirtied.

The first chapter of *The Man Without Qualities* is headed, "Which, remarkably enough, does not get anyone anywhere". For the whole *k.k.* world—the decadent *Käiserlich-Königlich*, Imperial-Royal autocracy—Musil coined the word "Kakania". His account of that world is a famous piece of writing: "There, in Kakania, the misunderstood State that has since vanished, which was in so many things a model though all unacknowledged, there was speed . . . but not too much speed. Whenever one thought of that country from some place abroad, the memory that hovered before the eyes was of wide, white, prosperous roads dating from the age of foot-travellers and mail-coaches. . . . Of course cars also drove along those roads—but not too many cars! The conquest of the air had begun here too; but not too intensively. Now and then a ship was sent off to South America or the Far East; but not too often. There was no ambition to have world markets and world power. . . . One spent tremendous sums on the army; but only just enough to assure one of remaining the second weakest among the great powers.

"The capital, too, was somewhat smaller than all the rest of the world's largest cities, but nevertheless quite considerably larger than a mere ordinary large city. And the administration of this country was carried out in an enlightened, hardly perceptible manner, with a cautious clipping of all sharp points, by the best bureaucracy in Europe, which could be accused of only one defect: it could not help regarding genius and enterprise of genius in private persons, unless privileged by high birth or State appointment, as ostentation, indeed presumption. But who would want unqualified persons putting their oar in, anyway? And besides, in Kakania it was only that a genius was always regarded as a lout, but never, as sometimes happened elsewhere, that a mere lout was regarded as a genius."

What better elegy for the Habsburgs? Even as he was writing, Musil was filled with nostalgia for what he railed against. That is why he has more dimension that the destructive Kraus or the opportunistic Almas and Bertas of the salons and coffee-houses. One of Musil's favourite images, as the translators of *The Man Without Qualities* noted in an introduction, was that of Man "irresistibly attracted by the sweet smell of life, as the fly is by that of the fly-paper, and each is doomed, with every moment of attempted escape, to sink a little deeper, so perishing in the sweet stickiness". It was absurd to pretend that life in Kakania had not been sweet and sticky. Kakania had been admirable, Musil knew perfectly well, in its easy-going attitudes, its colourfulness, its family life, the sense of muddling through from one contradiction to another. And Kakania had been appalling, like other autocratic states, in its poverty, its indifference to wasting diseases in the masses, its injustices. But to change was to run appalling risks. Kakania had to be admired in the main, but it was too late to prevent its destruction. No wonder that very few of the intelligent people were capable of taking action in the face of that dilemma. They waited until the dilemma overtook them, and Kakania and Old Vienna were no more.

A wedding party strikes an odd note of sartorial decorum amid the turmoil of the Volksprater's amusements.

Volksprater Pleasures

Vienna's least formal locus of leisure is the Volksprater funfair, a coruscating neon playland located at the northern tip of the Prater park and frequented by Viennese of all ages. By day it serves as a mechanized recreation area for children and their watchful parents. Dusk brings a different world.

Young factory and office workers out for excitement are lured by its whirligigs, roller coasters and dive-bombers—as well as such recent innovations as sex exhibits and striptease booths. Loudspeakers rend the night with over-amplified pop music, the air is sharp with the scent of hot snacks and cheap perfume, and the sky becomes a phantasmagoria of naked lights and whirling circles of colour.

The lights of electronic carousels and a giant rotor spangle the skyline of the amusement park at dusk.

A paprika-haired girl bites into a lingos—a Hungarian snack of fried dough sprinkled with garlic.

Oblivious to the lurid façade and open door of an adults-only "sex museum", a lone passer-by hurries homeward through the Volksprater on a rainy afternoon.

The two decades following the end of the First World War were bleak and uncertain in Vienna. Gustav Klimt, most gifted of the Secessionists, died young in 1918, and so did his most promising successor, the young painter Egon Schiele. Klimt had a stroke, and Schiele was a victim of the Spanish influenza epidemic which followed the war. In 1922, Adolf Loos drifted off to Paris. The writer Franz Werfel left Vienna with his Alma in 1938 and drifted from country to country. Just before Germany annexed Austria, Musil delivered a lecture in Vienna titled *On Stupidity*, criticizing the Nazis, and he then emigrated, to die in Switzerland. Musicians like Arnold Schoenberg and the conductor Bruno Walter also left to finish their careers in the United States.

The philosopher Ludwig Wittgenstein, perhaps the most original of them all, suffered from the dilemma of not knowing what to do or where to go. He was the son of one of the richest industrialists in Austria, who had prospered in the First World War. Wittgenstein's attitude towards this wealth was ambiguous, in that he gave his own share back to his family in order to assert his independence but then went to live with them in their palace on the Argentinierstrasse. But restlessness took over. In the 1920s he was by turns a teacher in a peasant school in the country and an architect in Vienna, but neither experiment was a success. Already he had spent long lonely stretches by himself in Norway; finally, in 1929, he fled to Cambridge University in England, and to philosophy. In his lifetime he published only his *Tractatus*, the basis of his great reputation.

Like Kraus, Wittgenstein thought that language held the clues to universal riddles, but he was not confident that anything could be expressed meaningfully. In Cambridge, he was a legendary eccentric, known for his enjoyment of cowboy stories and silent films. How appropriate it is that one of the last Viennese accepted by his peers to be a genius should also have been an enigma. Whatever statements he makes in his published work, he seems also to withdraw, as if unable to be positive about anything—a perfect engine, so to speak, harnessed to no frame. What a symbol for the way Vienna simply came to a stop.

The stage had been left to other sons of Austria: Hitler; Ernst Kaltenbrunner, the head of the Sicherheitsdienst (the Security Section of the Gestapo); Adolf Eichmann, the bureaucrat who organized the transports to the death camps; Franz Stangl, commandant of the camps of Treblinka and Sobibor, before whose eyes 400,000 people were exterminated; specialists in mass-murder like Odilo Globocnik and Dieter Wisliceny and their minions, tens of thousands of them Austrian—a far higher proportion of the population than their fellow murderers in the German Reich. They murdered with a vengeance, these dispossessed citizens of Kakania, proud to obliterate the sense of their own history. They had felt the tensions of the Gay Apocalypse too, and embraced them for the sake of death.

To point that out in Vienna is to risk a row. There must be few places in the free world that so assiduously and skilfully avoid looking themselves in the eye. But the city has had a reminder: Simon Wiesenthal. After the Second World War he forbade the complete Viennese flight from reality and, for that reason, was resented. He dedicated his life to bringing former Nazi criminals to justice; and that activity alone shattered illusions and brought people up short to confront facts. He himself went through 13 concentration camps and twice escaped summary execution only by the greatest good fortune.

In the years after 1960, Wiesenthal organized the Documentation Centre, a one-man office in an anonymous Viennese flat crammed with files and records. He became an avenging angel, accumulating all the evidence for Judgement Day, convinced that moral degeneracy as it afflicted Europe could be arrested. Volunteers and well-wishers around the world helped him with his self-appointed task. Eventually he could claim a role in capturing Adolf Eichmann as well as hunting down Franz Stangl in Brazil. In time more than 3,000 Nazis would be prosecuted as a result of Wiesenthal's work.

In his youth, Wiesenthal must have had a fine physique. When I last saw him in 1975, he was approaching 70 and was still fighting fit. His expressive brown eyes missed nothing.

"If I have a satisfaction," he told me, "it is that, when two Nazis quarrel, one says to the other, 'I will go to Wiesenthal and tell him all about you'; and you know, he usually does."

In modern Austria, he said, the block of former Nazis was still nearly half a million strong—the S.S. men and possible criminals among them numbering perhaps 10,000; and their electoral and political influence was significant. He also made the point, which he said was central to the moral climate of Vienna, that whereas the Germans had made such reparations as they could to their victims, the Austrians had done nothing at all, arguing that the responsibility was not theirs; but, of course, the city had been an important Nazi centre in its own right.

I asked him how the local authorities viewed his work. Well, they had tried to run him out of town. They had failed.

Here was a conscience not to be stilled. Wiesenthal was doing for his time what Freud had done in his: drawing attention to hypocrisy, shattering the social codes that have been elaborated to cover up the unfortunate realities. Wiesenthal was a *memento mori.*

Still, he would never pierce through the wilful refusal to come to terms with the real past. Who wants to live with reproaches when he can set his ambitions on shiny BMWs and Mercedes, and skiing vacations and summers beside a mountain lake? Why bother with the death camp at Mauthausen, located along the autobahn from Vienna, when there are charter flights to the Maldive Islands? The Viennese go about their

The glass-and-concrete office complex known as United Nations City towers over eastern Vienna, providing room for 4,500 U.N. civil servants. The complex, here photographed in 1977 as it neared completion, symbolizes Austria's post-war identity as a neutral state.

business by courtesy of selective memories. They contrive to slip through the mesh of the past; they do not care to make reflections upon the thorny questions about the end of the Gay Apocalypse.

Vienna today is a kind of painful collage: on the one hand, modernistic blocks and skyscrapers for the United Nations or organizations with acronyms like UNCTAD and OPEC, and on the other, a waxworks show of bygone glories, architectural and historical. In acting as hosts to the international community, the Viennese hope to find a new sense of purpose, but their natural inclination is to look to their past for salvation in matters big and small. For example, what other city has laid just over three miles of new tram tracks in the 1970s? There are no conductors on the trams; you are on your honour to pay for a ticket, and you do because that is integral to the old code of decent behaviour.

In winter, huge black crows perch, motionless on the branches of the trees along the tram line. In the evening, or in the winter half-light, electric sparks crackle off the overhead conductor wires of the trams. In summer, the air carries soft scents. At dusk neon signs light up, huge and forbidding, on the parapets of buildings: Kosmos, Donau, Allianz, Victoria, Phoenix, Merkur—insurance companies and banks and breweries—beacons of this last outpost of Western Europe. The neighbouring Communist countries out there in the dark have denied and renounced their past in the name of a hypothetical future. Very little is left to tie them to their history. Vienna exaggerates the other way, mortgaging the present for its hypothetical past.

Sunday visitors (right) follow a shaded avenue through Vienna's 470-acre Central Cemetery, some of them coming to tend family graves, others to stroll among the memorials of greater and lesser figures from the city's past. Even so minor a personage as a bygone supplier of pianos to the Emperor Franz Josef rates a splendid memorial (above), complete with a marble keyboard and a bronze figure who seems deeply moved by unheard music.

Stand on the steps of Loos's "house without eyebrows" on the Michaelerplatz and you will read on the wall a plaque to commemorate Oberfeuerwerker (Master Gunner) Johann Pollet, who on this spot refused to open fire on the workers and students during the uprising of 1848. Opposite, on the wall of the Palais Wilczek is a plaque to the effect that the poet Eichendorff and the dramatist Grillparzer lived there in the 19th Century. Around the corner by the Michaelerkirche is a plaque for the 18th-Century poet Metastasio who lived and died on the square, and yet another, next to it, dedicated to Haydn, who once had rooms there. Twenty yards farther along the Kohlmarkt is a plaque noting that Chopin spent a winter there. It can get a person down to be wandering through this glorious necropolis; his footprint is so puny in comparison with their mighty tread.

In the Minoritenkloster—the Monastry of the Minorites—opposite the old hospital on the Alserstrasse, the cloisters are decorated with little, oblong marble plaques about 12 inches by eight. Each of them is a prayer to St. Anthony, and each is also a cry from the heart, from someone in distress: "Please, send me back my missing husband, May 4, 1944"; "Toni, who on 10.9.1941 found a hero's death at Smolensk"; "Keep our Franzi under your protection"; "Maria Hawliczek, born in Brünn

22.7.1865, died on the painful journey from her homeland on 28.6.1945". The years 1918 and 1945 were times of crescendo for these plaques. What all of them amount to is that unstoppable, heart-felt plea of the individual down all ages, to be left alone to make his fate. Franzi, Toni, Maria Hawliczek, and thousands recorded in this cloister were born when the times were out of joint. In one sense, each of these plaques is a selfish demand; in another sense, each is a devout hope to be in peace, with loved ones, unbothered by the commotion of a frightening world.

Of the million or so Austrians who have settled abroad, some as refugees but others to make their way in the world, an astonishingly high proportion return to die, or at least are brought back for burial in the family plot, which is usually the one heirloom surviving when all else has been lost. Vienna is rich in cemeteries, all of them carefully tended and an essential part of the culture. Large sums are paid for the entrée to the right ones; people scrimp during a life-time for the privilege of lying alongside the respected dead, as opposed to any old body.

There is no getting away from the dead, no discreet disposal of those whose work is over and done with. On the contrary, the cemeteries are miniatures of the city, with smart and shabby sections, outmoded patches of overcrowding, or exclusive "green belts" where the grass is neat and short. And discrimination is preserved beyond the grave. Catholics, Protestants and Jews are buried each in their sections and religious styles, and each according to their means. The rich lie side by side in mausoleums as splendid as their Ringstrasse palaces once were, flanked by sorrowful statuary, gothicky tracery, sculptural ornament to suit their rank. Nobody seems too poor for marble.

A person's occupation or achievements must be blazoned in gilded letters for eternity—or, more specifically, for anyone who happens to be passing by during eternity. The inscriptions on a tombstone will declare with pith what amount of respect is due to the departed: *"Privatier und Hausbesitzer"*, a Man of Property and House-owner. *"Restaurateurs-gattin"*, Wife of a Restaurant Proprietor. *"k.k. Kassa Director"*, an Accountant with the civil service. *"Präsident des Verwaltungsrates der k.k. Priv. Lemberg-Czernowitz-Jassy Eisenbahn"*, President of a Provincial Railway administrative board. *"Äusserste Waise eines k.k. Obersts"*, Eldest Orphan of a Colonel—the lady so described had died in her eighties. All these people must have wanted to guarantee that they would be launched socially just where they left off, in case the resurrection of the flesh led to any misconceptions.

What happened to Mozart, it will be realized now, was as horrible as it could have been, outright proof of his failure and rejection in Vienna. Mozart died virtually abandoned by friends and patrons of any consequence. The cheapest possible funeral was ordered, for nobody was prepared to come forward and pay expenses. The service was held outside St. Stefan's, since paupers did not rate a service inside, and the untended, unaccompanied hearse then drove away to St. Marx's cemetery, outside the walls. Not one mourner was on hand for the burial. The coffin was dumped into a common grave, the ultimate indignity which the city reserved for its poor. To this day nobody knows the site of Mozart's grave, but St. Marx's has been kitted up, long posthumously, with a makeshift memorial and a pretty cherub beside it. Too late, too false.

Other illustrious dead such as Beethoven and Johann Strauss are in the Zentralfriedhof in Simmering, and though on two or three occasions I have followed the arrows to their *Ehrengräber*, or Graves of Honour, the area is so vast that I have always lost my way. The cemetery covers 750 acres, large enough for the administration to organize a shoot there each November to keep down the hares and the deer browsing among the colonnades, cloisters, clipped hedges, obelisks, and even around the huge pantheon of a church in the centre. Instead of Beethoven and Strauss, the best memorial I have discovered is *k.u.k. Feldmarschall* Svetozar Baron Boroevič von Bojna, hero of the battles of the Isonzo on the Italian front in the First World War, the last military engagements won by the Austrians. The field-marshal died on May 23, 1920, but the Austrian Republic's army of today still maintains a grateful wreath with patriotic red and white ribbons attached to it.

And the Habsburgs? From 1600 to the present, they have been buried in their private crypt under the Capuchin church in the very centre of Vienna (though their hearts, macabre touch, are preserved near by in the Augustinerkirche). Franz Josef still has a pair of wreaths with red and white ribbons laid on his tomb every year.

I attend the funeral of an old friend. The florist asks what coloured ribbons I want to attach to my bunch of flowers—black, white, purple, or yellow? It is a brilliant January day, but five degrees below freezing, with snow hard as icing sugar. In the Baroque chapel of Hietzing cemetery, there is no heating. The choristers who sing the requiem are blue with cold. So is the monsignor from St. Stefan's who gives the eulogy. Then four figures in astonishing blue-grey uniforms, buttoned up and hatted like honorary soldiers, carry out the coffin to the family vault; these four undertakers are known as *Pompfinewarer*, a typical borrowing from the French (*pompes-funèbres*).

The mourners stand in line to throw a little shovelful of earth upon the lowered coffin. The *Pompfinewarer* who hands us the shovel also has tiny bunches of flowers to throw down too, and he must be tipped well for his services: *"Man kauft sich vom Tod los"*, as the phrase goes—"One is buying off death". We shake hands and depart, murmuring that our old friend has made a *"schöne Leich'"*, a beautiful funeral. That was the point of it all, then.

A Population of Stone

From her watery perch in the Naiad Fountain, a reclining river nymph anxiously gazes skyward at rainclouds casting a fine drizzle over Schönbrunn Park.

The past is never far away in Vienna—often, in fact, no further than the nearest square or garden, where the spirit of some bygone age is likely to be embodied in sculptural form. The city's heritage of statuary is exceptionally rich. Much of it dates from the 18th Century, when noblemen commissioned legions of angels and figures from classical mythology to decorate their palace terraces and lend interest to their private parks. The massive urban renewal projects of the 19th Century made room for a new array of historical allegories and monuments to statesmen and artists, while the 20th Century has added art nouveau nudes and other modernist works. At times the statues seem to be almost animate, as though forming a secondary population—reminders to the living of the greatness of the Viennese dead.

A crow provides an audience for a lute-player disfigured by snow—one of six sculptures of musicians lining the central avenue of the Belvedere Palace garden.

A mantle of vine leaves serves to protect the modesty of a wreath-bearing art nouveau nude in one of the corner towers of the Burggarten hothouses.

The grimace of a vanquished sea-god, part of an allegorical statue depicting Habsburg naval power, fails to alarm two ladies sightseeing in the Michaelerplatz.

In the Schwarzenberg Garden, a girl skips past two statues by the Italian artist Lorenzo Mattielli depicting the Rape of the Sabine Women.

Under the stern gaze of one of the sphinxes ornamenting steps in the Belvedere Palace garden, a little girl rushes for safety to a relative's raincoat.

In the square that bears her name, a monument to the 18th-Century Empress Maria Theresa looms beyond a traffic light's illustrated injunction to pedestrians.

Bibliography

Allmayer-Beck and Lessing, *Die K. & K. Armée 1848-1914.* C. Bertelsmann Verlag, Gütersloh, 1974.
Anderson, Emily (ed.), *The Letters of Beethoven.* Macmillan London Ltd., London, 1961.
Anderson, Emily (ed.), *Letters of Mozart and his family.* Macmillan London Ltd., London, 1958.
Bader, William B., *Austria Between East and West 1945-1955.* Stanford University Press, Stanford, 1966.
Barea, Ilse, *Vienna, Legend and Reality.* Martin Secker & Warburg, London, 1966.
Barker, Elisabeth, *Austria 1918-1942.* The Macmillan Press Ltd., London, 1973.
Brion, Marcel, *Daily Life in the Vienna of Mozart and Schubert.* Weidenfeld & Nicolson, London, 1961.
Brook-Shepherd, Gordon, *Anschluss.* Macmillan & Co. Ltd., London, 1963.
Brook-Shepherd, Gordon, *The Austrian Odyssey.* Macmillan London Ltd., London, 1957.
Brook-Shepherd, Gordon, *The Last Habsburg.* Weidenfeld & Nicolson, London, 1968.
Crankshaw, Edward, *The Habsburgs.* Weidenfeld & Nicolson, London, 1971.
Crankshaw, Edward, *Vienna, 2nd edition.* Macmillan London Ltd., London, 1976.
Cross, Milton, *Encyclopedia of the Great Composers.* Doubleday & Company Inc., New York, 1962.
Elon, Amos, *Herzl.* Weidenfeld & Nicolson, London, 1975.
Freud, Sigmund, *The Psychopathology of Everyday Life.* Penguin Books Ltd., Harmondsworth, 1975.
Geretsegger H., Peintner M. (eds.), *Wagner, Otto, 1841-1918.* Residenz Verlag, Salzburg, 1964.
Goimard, Jacques (ed.), *Vienne au temps de François-Joseph.* Réalités Hachette, Paris, 1970.
Habe, Hans, *Wien, so wie es war.* Droste Verlag, Düsseldorf, 1969.
Hauenstein, Hans, *Wiener Dialekt.* Karl & Otto Karner, Vienna, 1974.
Heer, Friedrich, *God's First Love.* Weidenfeld & Nicolson, London, 1967.
Henderson, Nicholas, *Prince Eugene of Savoy.* Weidenfeld & Nicolson, London, 1964.
Hennings, Fred, *Das Barocke Wien.* Herold Verlag, Vienna, 1965.
Hennings, Fred, *Ringstrassensymphonie (3 vols.).* Herold Verlag, Vienna, 1963.
Hubmann, Franz, *K. & K. Familienalbum.* Fritz Molden Verlag, Vienna-Munich-Zurich, 1971.
Janik, Allen & Toulmin, S., *Wittgenstein's Vienna.* Weidenfeld & Nicolson, London, 1973.
Jenks, W. A., *Vienna and the Young Hitler.* Oxford University Press, Oxford, 1960.
Johnston, William M., *The Austrian Mind.* University of California Press, London, 1972.
Jones, Ernest, *The Life and Work of Sigmund Freud.* The Hogarth Press, London, 1961.
Kralik, Heinrich, *Das Grosse Orchester.* W. Frick, Vienna, 1952.
Kralik, Heinrich, *The Vienna Opera House.* Verlag Brüder Rosenbaum, Vienna, 1955.
Kreisler, Fritz, *Four Weeks in the Trenches.* Houghton, Mifflin & Co., 1915.
Langer, William L., *An Encyclopedia of World History.* George G. Harrap & Co. Ltd., London, 1968.
Leitich, Ann Tizia, *The Spanish Riding School in Vienna.* Nymphenburger Verlagshandlung, Munich, 1956.
Lernet-Holenia, A., *H. Qualtinger und sein Wien.* Vorstadt Europas, 1963.
Macartney, C. A., *The Habsburg Empire.* Weidenfeld & Nicolson, London, 1969.
Mahler, Alma, *Gustav Mahler.* John Murray Ltd., London, 1968.
Mahler, Alma, *And the Bridge is Love.* Harcourt, Brace, Jovanovich Ltd., London, 1958.
Mannoni, O., *Freud.* New Left Books, New York, 1971.
Musil, Robert, *The Man Without Qualities.* Martin Secker & Warburg Ltd., London, 1953.
Musulin, Stella, *Vienna in the Age of Metternich.* Faber & Faber, London, 1975.
Pick, Robert, *The Last Days of Imperial Vienna.* Weidenfeld & Nicolson, London, 1975.
Powell, Nicholas, *The Sacred Spring.* Studio Vista, London, 1974.
Prawy, Marcel, *Vienna Opera.* Praeger Publications, New York, 1970.
Rieff, Philip, *Freud—The Mind of a Moralist.* Victor Gollancz, London, 1960.
Roth, Ernst, *A Tale of Three Cities.* Cassell & Company Ltd., London, 1971.
Schnitzler, Arthur, *My Youth in Vienna.* Weidenfeld & Nicolson, London, 1971.
Schonberg, Harold C., *The Lives of the Great Composers.* Futura Publications Ltd., London, 1975.
Spiel, Hilde (ed.), *Wien Spektrum einer Stadt.* Biederstein Verlag, Munich, 1971.
Stoye, J. W., *The Siege of Vienna.* Collins, London, 1964.
Torberg, Friedrich, *Die Tante Jolesch.* Langen Müller, Munich, 1975.
Trollope, Frances, *Vienna and the Austrians.* Bentley, London, 1838.
Vergo, Peter, *Art in Vienna.* Phaidon Press Ltd., London, 1975.
Wagner, Dieter and Tomkowitz, Gerhard, *Ein Volk, Ein Reich, Ein Führer.* Longman Group Ltd., London, 1971.
Wagner, Richard, *My Life.* Constable & Company Ltd., London, 1911.
Wagner-Rieger, Renate (ed.), *Die Wiener Ringstrasse, Vols. 1-9.* Franz Steiner Verlag, Wiesbaden, 1969-1976.
Wangermann, Ernst, *The Austrian Achievement.* Thames & Hudson Ltd., London, 1973.
Wechsberg, Joseph, *Sounds of Vienna.* Weidenfeld & Nicolson, London, 1968.
Wechsberg, Joseph, *The Waltz Emperors.* Weidenfeld & Nicolson, London, 1973.
Williams, C. E., *The Broken Eagle.* Paul Elek, London, 1974.
Zweig, Stefan, *The World of Yesterday.* Cassell & Company Ltd., London, 1943.
Vienna Tourist Board (ed.), *Vienna Present and Past.* Jugend und Volk Verlagsgesellschaft mbH, Vienna, 1974.
Zeman, Z. A. B., *Twilight of the Habsburgs.* BPC Unit 75, London, 1971.

Credits and Acknowledgements

The author and editors wish to thank the following for their valuable assistance:

Austrian Institute, London; Charles Dettmer, Thames Ditton, Surrey; Dr. R. J. W. Evans, Brazenose College, Oxford; Martha Foite, City of Vienna Press Office, Vienna; Susan Goldblatt, London; Hunting Surveys Ltd., London; Wolfgang J. Kraus, Fremdenverkehrsverband für Wien, Vienna; Elizabeth Loving, London; J. S. Lucas, Imperial War Museum, London; Dr. Charles Rycroft, London; David Sinclair, London; Hugo Williams, London; Giles Wordsworth, Dorset.

Sources for pictures in this book are shown below. Credits for the pictures from left to right are separated by commas; from top to bottom they are separated by dashes.

All photographs are by Thomas Höpker except: Page 7—Gunn Brinson. 10, 11, 12—Bildarchiv Öst. Nationalbibliothek, Vienna. 13—Radio Times Hulton Picture Library. 14, 15—Map by Hunting Surveys Ltd., London. Silhouettes by Norman Bancroft-Hunt. 26, 27—Historisches Museum der Stadt Wien, Vienna. 32—Gunn Brinson. 44, 45—F. Wolfsberger from Zefa, London. 47—Historisches Museum der Stadt Wien, Vienna. 56—Radio Times Hulton Picture Library, London. 59—Radio Times Hulton Picture Library, London. 60, 61—Heeresgeschichtliches Museum, Vienna. 64, 65—Bildarchiv Öst. Nationalbibliothek, Vienna—bottom row centre—Coll. J. S. Lucas. 78, 79—Erich Lessing from Magnum, Paris. 87—Historisches Museum der Stadt Wien, Vienna. 114—Sigmund Freud Copyrights Ltd., Colchester. 116—Coll. Prof. Heinrich Schnitzler. 117-119—Sigmund Freud Copyrights Ltd., Colchester. 125—Bildarchiv Öst Nationalbibliothek, Vienna. 132—Historisches Museum der Stadt Wien, Vienna. 146—(right) Gunn Brinson. 148, 149—Historisches Museum der Stadt Wien, Vienna. 164—Victor Fogarassy, Graz. 167—Historisches Museum der Stadt Wien, Vienna. 169—Historisches Museum der Stadt Wien, Vienna/Galerie Welz, Salzburg. 170, 171—David Brinson. 174—Bildarchiv Öst. Nationalbibliothek, Vienna. 175—Gunn Brinson.

Quotation on page 6 from *The Third Man* by Graham Greene reproduced by kind permission of William Heinemann Ltd.
Quotations on pages 10 and 122 from *The World of Yesterday* by Stefan Zweig reproduced by kind permission of Cassell & Company Ltd.
Quotation on page 44 from *Drunt in Der Lobau* © Heinrich Strecker, Baden-bei-Wien, Austria.
Quotation on page 93 from *Sounds of Vienna* by Joseph Wechsberg reproduced by kind permission of Weidenfeld & Nicolson.
Quotation on pages 118 and 126 from *Freud, The Man, His World, His Influence,* edited by Jonathan Miller, reproduced by kind permission of Weidenfeld & Nicolson.
Quotation on page 121 from *"Wien, Stadt meiner Träume",* music and words by Rudolf Sieczynski, © Adolf Robithscek, Piaristengasse 12-14, Vienna.
Quotation on page 127 from *"Es wird ein Wein sein",* music by Ludwig Gruber, words by Josef Hornig, published by Bosworth, London, Cologne and Vienna.
Quotation on page 127 from *"Zehn Schillings für die Schrammelmusik",* © Theodor Wottitz.
Quotation on page 130 from *My Life* by Richard Wagner reproduced by kind permission of Constable & Company Ltd.
Quotation on page 171 from *And the Bridge is Love* by Alma Mahler reproduced by kind permission of Harcourt, Brace, Jovanovich, Inc.
Quotation on page 176 from *The Man Without Qualities* by Robert Musil, translated by Eithne Wilkins and Ernst Kaiser, reproduced by kind permission of Martin Secker & Warburg Ltd.

Index

Numerals in italics indicate a photograph or drawing of the subject mentioned.

Colour reproduction by Irwin Photography Ltd., at their Leeds PDI Scanner Studio.
Filmsetting by C. E. Dawkins (Typesetters) Ltd., London, SE1 1UN.
Printed and bound in Italy by Arnoldo Mondadori, Verona.